Complete Digital Illustration

Complete Digital Illustration

A Master Class in Image-Making

Lawrence Zeegen

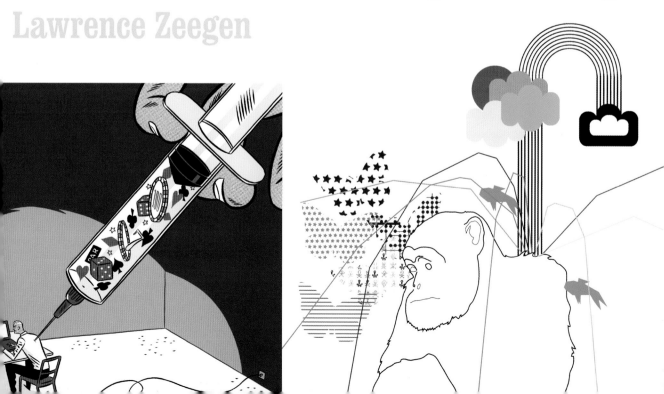

A RotoVision Book

Published and distributed by RotoVision SA
Route Suisse 9
CH-1295 Mies
Switzerland

RotoVision SA
Sales and Editorial Office
Sheridan House, 114 Western Road
Hove BN3 1DD, UK

Tel: +44 (0)1273 72 72 68
Fax: +44 (0)1273 72 72 69
www.rotovision.com

10 9 8 7 6 5 4 3 2 1

ISBN: 978-2-88893-096-9

Art Directors: Luke Herriott and Tony Seddon
Design: Russell Hrachovec, Ondrej Slezek, and
Benoît Schmit at compoundEye
Picture research by Ondrej Slezek

Reprographics in Singapore by ProVision Pte.
Tel: +65 6334 7720
Fax: +65 6334 7721

Printed in China by 1010 Printing International Ltd.

NOW WHERE DID
I PUT COLIN?

Contents

Introduction

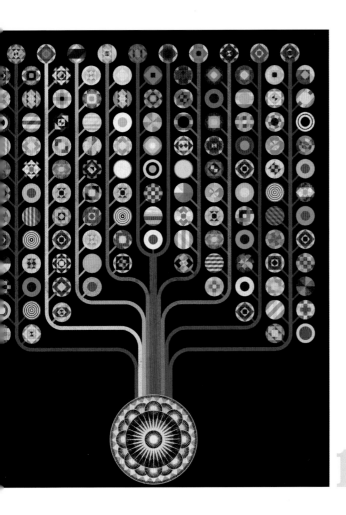

Adapt or die

This book takes up the story from the point in the digital revolution at which technology has given way to creativity, the balance of power having shifted in favor of the big idea.

It wasn't always this way. Before the digital revolution, life as an illustrator was fairly straightforward—or so it seemed. There was no Apple, no Photoshop, no Google—no Internet, no e-mail, no hassle. Looking back at life before the revolution, albeit through rose-tinted glasses, the working day for your lone illustrator was a fairly simple affair.

In the precomputer age, a common-or-garden commission for a freelance illustrator would come about through a phone call made by an art director to an illustrator's landline. Cell phones only came into everyday use in the 1990s. If you were out of the studio when the call came, chances were you would miss the job. Even in 1990, answer phones were not the norm, and the brief itself would have to be posted or collected: fax machines were huge, cumbersome, and expensive items. Without websites and e-mail, illustrators utilized the humble postcard as their calling card to the creative world, designing, printing, addressing, and posting hundreds of these mail shots on a regular basis. With just that single postcard to judge an illustrator by, art directors took time out of their working day to view physical portfolios. Yes, they would actually look at real work, in real time, in the real world. In the early years of the twenty-first century, those who commission illustration can view work in seconds, make creative decisions in minutes, have an illustrator briefed within hours, and set deadlines of a few days. The means by which freelance illustrators maintain a professional profile, inform clients of new work, and show their portfolios have altered beyond recognition.

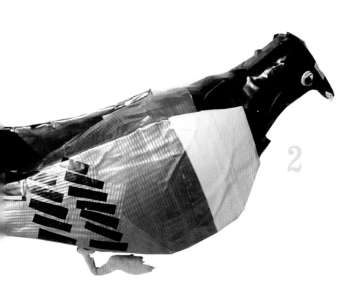

1. Christian Montenegro, *New Scientist* magazine, "Mr Hawking's Flexiverse," editorial.

2. Holly Wales, *Sellotape Pigeon*, personal project.

3. Adrian Johnson, 2K By Gingham, Inspire T-shirt design.

Gazing into the future back in 1992, John Warwicker, Creative Director of design collective Tomato, said, without even a trace of irony, "I can envisage a time when we'll all need our own individual Macs." The digital revolution took no prisoners. It was clear—adapt or die! Accordingly, the working life, lifestyles, and life skills needed by today's "creatives" have altered, and accelerated.

From analogue to digital

Jason Ford, Association of Illustrators award winner, entered the industry with a purely traditional skill set. Ford recalls his own transition into the digital realm. "My work had always been about trying to achieve a flat graphic/silk-screen feel," he explains. "I was trying to hide the brush mark as much as I could." Moving from brush and paint to screen and mouse wasn't seamless though.

"People kept telling me I could achieve what I was doing with paint so much more easily and quickly using a computer, but of course I resisted this as long as possible," he recalls. "For me, back then, the digital world was a void of incomprehensible gibberish!"

Also leaving college at the end of the 1980s was textile designer turned collage artist, turned illustrator/designer Paul Burgess, best known at the time for his seminal book jackets for Vintage. "When computers came along in the mid-1990s," recalls Burgess, "we all hated them. We thought they were rubbish. We were all proved so wrong!"

Recognizing that technology was in flux, that everything was poised to change, Burgess embraced digital technology, but in his own, punk-inspired fashion. "I bought my first Mac and slowly started to grasp Photoshop, but trying to misuse it as much as possible," he admits. It is clear that some entered the digital domain on their own terms.

Entry into the digital world came at a price. "My first Mac cost nearly £3,000 [c. US $5,000]. Crazy when you think about it now. And it was so very slow," says Burgess. Buying and setting up a Mac was at the bottom of a new and radically steep learning curve. Getting to grips with software, even if you could master the hardware, would be a challenge to those who had always worked manually. "I'm self-taught," admits Burgess, "with loads of help from mates who have begrudgingly shown me tricks along the way."

Jason Ford concurs with Burgess. "I've always had loads of help from studio buddies a lot further down the digital path than me. It helps to share studio space with designers who understand all the technical stuff and can help out when an image disappears from your screen for no reason at all!"

LOVES TO SCRATCH

SAVE THE TAPE

13

An education in illustration

For a younger generation of illustrators and image-makers, the digital revolution kicked in during their time at art school, not that institutions were quick to respond, or face the challenges ahead. Lucy Vigrass (original Peepshow crew) graduated in 1998. "I think we had a one-day session in Photoshop," she recalls. "We made pictures of ourselves looking like we had clingfilm [plastic wrap] over our faces!" Keen to embrace new working methods and techniques, Vigrass learnt the hard way. "Most of my learning came from people around me and working things out myself. You pick things up out of necessity and shortcut one-upmanship."

Brett Ryder, emerging in the mid-1990s, wasn't equipped any more ably than Vigrass. "I learnt to use the computer at home," he recalls. "At the time most of the people using the computer at college were graphic design students, so I didn't get the help I needed." As well as getting the right kind of teaching, getting in front of the kit was problematic. At the time, Ryder's work, now a unique blend of collage with hand- and digitally rendered drawing and painting, wasn't going anywhere. "I was unhappy with the direction my work was taking, so I turned to the computer. I thought it could help solve the aesthetic problems I was experiencing." Ryder now works regularly for clients across the globe, recently for the *New York Times*, the *Daily Telegraph*, *GQ* magazine, and *O, the Oprah Magazine*. "The degree in which I draw or collage, and my use of the digital know-how, fluctuates as I progress my work," Ryder explains, but his working methods have changed little.

John McFaul graduated in 1996. Today, no stranger to the pages of *Computer Arts*, he can visit his past with humor and a touch of nostalgia. "I'm mainly self-taught," he explains. "Graduating in the dark ages meant that computers were the tools 'of the designers,' but because I've always been influenced by design, far more so than illustration, they always held some intrigue," he adds.

Knowing just how far he has come, McFaul muses on an early job. "I remember the first job I did using Photoshop. It was terrible! I barely knew how to use any of the tools and I was ringing my 'designer' friends every five minutes with questions."

13. Joe McLaren, The Lodge, *Piece of Cake,* album cover.

14. Kerry Roper, Nike, Air Jordan T-Shirt design.

15. Brett Ryder, the *Telegraph,* "Woman In A Man's World," editorial.

16. McFaul, *Mustplay* deck designs, personal project.

17. Yuko Kondo, Wieden+Kennedy, *Lucha Libre,* window display.

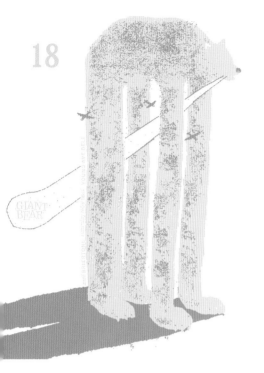

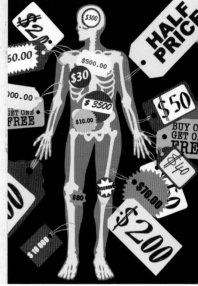

The digital generation

For those who have entered the creative industries, and more specifically the world of illustration, since the turn of this century, it would appear that everything has been digital for some considerable time. Advances in hardware and software have been enormous, and for a generation that has grown up with a PC in their bedroom, a cell phone in their pocket, and a playlist on their iPod, it is almost unthinkable that this technology wasn't around earlier than the 1990s.

Steve Wilson recalls his first foray into the digital world, fresh out of art school, in 2001. "I was commissioned to create eight thumbnail-sized illustrations for *The Guide*, the mag given away with the *Guardian* on a Saturday, and they were reproduced over a period of four weeks," he remembers. "I then didn't get another commission for nine months. I spent the money earned from the *Guardian* many times over during that period. But I've since worked for many clients, including Virgin, Coca-Cola, MTV, *Wallpaper**, and the BBC."

Self-taught, Wilson admits to never fully engaging with the digital while a student, and he is still learning. "I think I'm still only using a fraction of the software's capabilities," he explains. He gets what he needs from Illustrator and Photoshop, "but there are still plenty of tools and options I barely use," he admits. "Occasionally I'll discover something new and within a few months I'm thinking, 'how on Earth did I live without that!'"

Mr bingo considers himself "part of the digital generation. We started making images using computers at art school," he explains from his studio. "I've always been working digitally in a professional sense, but, of course, my induction was quite some time before." Not in the least reluctant to divulge his first brush with digital image-making, Mr bingo keenly recounts his proud past. "I was using Deluxe Paint III on the Commodore Amiga 500+ in the early '90s. I was making animations that simulated a few seconds of a scrolling shoot-'em-up, or the occasional flying penis. You know the kind of thing." We do?

Emily Alston, another fully paid-up member of the digital generation, having graduated from university in 2004, explains that the culture of her degree course actively encouraged digital working methods. "We had master classes at university, but as I had never really bracketed myself as an illustrator, I would leave my easel behind and follow the graphic designers into the IT suite," she explains.

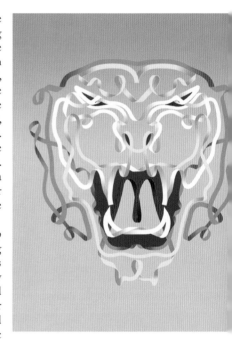

"There are still plenty of tools and options that I barely use. Occasionally I'll discover something new and within a few months I'm thinking, 'how on earth did I live without that!'"

18. Sasha Barr, Memphis, *Giant Bear* music poster.
19. Emily Alston, *Party*, personal project.
20. Lucy Vigrass, *TORO Magazine*, "Body Brokers," editorial.
21. Steve Wilson, Tank Theory, Ribbon Tiger T-shirt design.
22. Serge Seidlitz, MTV and Toonami, idents and logos.

23

24

Finding your own way

"It is important to find your own way of using technology. Illustrators and designers all have the same technology available to them. If everyone used the tools in the same way, nothing would ever stand out as different or original," Alston advises.

Paul Burgess, a generation apart from Alston, but in absolute agreement with her, states his case. "I think it's very difficult now. Everyone has a computer, everyone has the same software, and everyone thinks they can stick a couple of butterflies onto a twiddly background and they have an illustration. They don't have an illustration; they have decoration. There is a big difference! Digital technology is exciting, but only as exciting as the ideas you have inside your head."

"As with most professions," adds Jason Ford, drawing on his extensive experience, "75% of the illustration out there is a dog's dinner, but the other 25% keeps the standards high." Steve Wilson is a little more positive. "It is really all about trying to produce work that is distinctive and original, whatever that is. Work shouldn't be judged on the levels of technology involved in making it. I never understand people who are anticomputers or procomputers. Who really cares how you get the results. It's the final image that counts, regardless of how you got there." But Burgess demands the final word. "The idea is king. Once you have a strong idea, everything else just flows along behind it."

With fallout from the digital revolution now settled, interest has once again shifted back to ideas, back to what it is that makes an image work, to how the image communicates, and to what it has to say. Issues and debates are now more centered on an artist's own personal visual language than on software tips and tricks. Discussion about the illustration scene focuses on expressing a point of view rather than decorating a page. Today's top-notch digital illustrators maintain a balance of commercial and self-authored projects, motivated by the desire to communicate and to establish careers in an industry constantly under pressure from the whims of fashion.

> **"The idea is king. Once you have a strong idea, everything else just flows along behind it."**

25

Working Process

Creative Image-Making

Underground Influences

Bernard Edwards
RIP

It had to start somewhere. The recent upsurge of image-making within graphic design has its roots in aspects of youth culture.

An undercurrent of fresh, raw talent has always been responsible for forcing disciplines forward. Music, for example, was altered with the Sex Pistols and punk in the seventies and Public Enemy and hip-hop in the eighties; the landscape changed forever, as new music shed its past and reinvented itself by and for a new generation. Movies did the same in breaking the mold; *Easy Rider* in the sixties and *Mean Streets* in the seventies radically affected and influenced a new generation of filmmakers. In the arts, Andy Warhol in the sixties and Damien Hirst in the noughties have had a similar effect on popular culture and on their contemporaries.

Rejuvenation and Reinvention
For the graphic image-maker too, a rejuvenation and reinvention of the medium echoes the changes across aspects of popular culture. As new methods, approaches, fashions, and ideas merged with new technologies and new creative and commercial outlets, so new methods of working have begun to emerge. Finding or creating a platform for new work has always been tricky: the commercial world rarely wants to take risks, preferring to use a visual language that is tried and tested. Therefore, when an outlet that works as a test bed for visual innovation—maintaining and driving change—is created, it is vital to recognize its strengths.

Style Wars
It may seem long ago now, and the event has lost some of its significance, but the birth of the "style" magazine in the UK—with the publication of *The Face* in May 1980— was an important and defining moment in the recording, reporting, and reflection of a popular culture regarded as "of interest" by the nation's youth. Here was a template that would later be borrowed, copied, or pillaged, depending on your stance, around the world. Within just

3

4

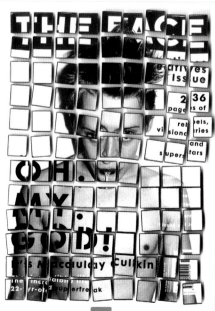

5

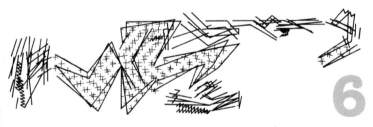

6

1. Billie Jean, *Native Weapon* magazine, Le Freak C'est Chic
2. Insect, Right Guard Xtreme Sport packaging
3. Andy Potts, Woodsuch Web site, Bubby 3-D
4. Insect, The Wooster Collective, Sin Clown
5. Walnut, *The Face* magazine, DeFace badges
6. Ian Wright, *The Face* magazine, Issue 01 Man

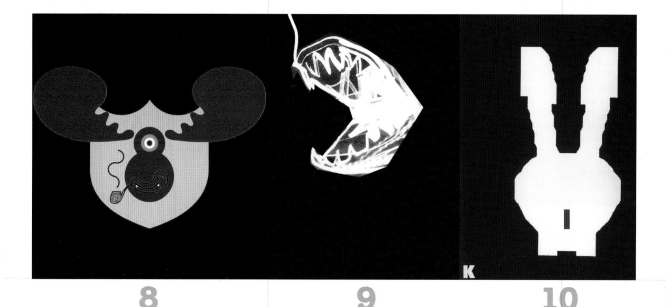

8   9   10

a few short years it was influencing not only others in magazine publishing, but also people across related fields including advertising, fashion, journalism, and design.

Design, and graphic design in particular, was high on the agenda in the era that dubbed itself The Designer Decade. It could be argued that it all began with that first issue of *The Face*, proclaiming itself "Numero Uno, licensed to thrill." Although the design was a little raw in places, it was clear that as well as reflecting popular youth culture, it would also play a part in defining it. Ahead of the British pack that was soon to include *i-D*, still going strong, and *Blitz* (a pale imitation of *The Face* that died a couple of years after its launch) the look and feel of *The Face* would go on to influence design in the US, notably in music magazines such as *Raygun*, and in the TV graphics for MTV.

7. Matthew Green, *Sleaze Nation* magazine, Ican'tbelieveitsnotbetter
8. Mick Marston, personal project, The Futile Vignette company exhibition, New York
9. Richard May, personal project, Carcharhinus leucas
10. Ian Wright, Tony Kaye, Bun Bun

The first issue of *The Face* featured just one image not created by the camera—a drawing by Ian Wright graced its contents page. The stark image of a zoot-suited man running, dancing, or perhaps chasing his hat, printed in simple black line, looked anything other than hand-drawn. Wright had produced an image which suggested that a computer had played some part in its creation. Jagged, edgy, almost digital in feel, though with a nod toward the work of Russian abstract artist Wassily Kandinsky, Wright's image looked both modern and youth-driven, with a hint of the digital, years before the technology would allow such work.

1984 and the Mac
The technology that would permit Wright and his contemporaries to start creating digital drawings was in its infancy at the dawn of the eighties. Apple, today widely regarded as the computer for creatives, had been set up in 1976 in California, but was yet to have an impact in the design world. However, in 1984, Apple announced the release of the first Macintosh range through its cinematic commercial "1984," directed by Ridley Scott. Only ever aired once, and that during the US Super Bowl, it immediately positioned Apple, with its advertising slogan: "the computer for the rest of us." With striking footage of a female athlete smashing a screen image of Big Brother, this stylish and emotive commercial helped Apple to play its own part in defining the visual esthetic of the decade. More importantly though, Apple had introduced the technology that would change the face of graphic design and image-making.

The Birth of Photoshop
It took a full three years for the Mac II, with the first color monitor, capable of displaying an impressive 256 colors. It took a further three years before the appearance of an early version of Photoshop, created for Adobe by brothers Thomas and John Knoll, following developments in the application that had originally started life as ImagePro. Photoshop's dominance had begun.

11

12

11. Rosie Irvine, Levi's/BBH, Blokes
12. Rosie Irvine, Levi's/BBH, Birds
13. Andy Martin, personal project, Studio Espresso 1985
14. Andy Martin, personal project, Web Man
15. Kidney, personal project, Death
16. Neasden Control Centre, group exhibition poster, LA: Beautiful Decay

mish mash
Sat 3rd January
at Cargo Kingsland Viaduct, 83 Rivington Street, Shoreditch, London, EC2

17

18

mish mash
Sat 1st November
at Cargo Kingsland Viaduct, 83 Rivington Street, Shoreditch, London, EC2

19

mish mash
Sat 6th March
at Cargo Kingsland Viaduct, 83 Rivington Street, Shoreditch, London, EC2

20

mish mash
Sat 3rd April
at Cargo Kingsland Viaduct, 83 Rivington Street, Shoreditch, London, EC2

17. Insect, Cargo, Mish Mash, poster
18. Insect, Cargo, Mish Mash, poster
19. Insect, Cargo, Mish Mash, poster
20. Insect, Cargo, Mish Mash, poster
21. Michael Gillette, *Spin* magazine, Radiohead

From the mid- to late eighties, designers and artists wishing to delve into digital practice faced numerous problems: the price of hardware was prohibitive, software was still complicated to use, and its functions were basic at best. Financial considerations ensured that the introduction of the digital into everyday working practices began in medium- to large-scale graphic design companies, but most small studios and freelance individuals did not have the capital for the set-up costs. This had a direct effect on the relationship that graphic design had with image-makers, who were predominantly solo or working within self-managed studio environments. In short, it was graphic design rather than image-making that took the lead. In 1992, John Warwicker, of design collective Tomato, said, "I can envisage a time when we'll all need our own individual Macs." Rewind just a short time and the digital world was a very different place from the one in which we live today.

Laser Light

Gradually, despite early difficulties, image-makers started to gain access to a new tool, one that would slowly introduce them to the notion of creating digital images. The Canon CLC, a color laser copier, provided the link between analog and digital methods of image creation for many. Early adopters of the CLC could resize originals, distort their shape, alter colors, create positives and negatives, and utilize an unprecedented range of image-manipulation tools. Andrew Coningsby, the man behind the illustration agency Debut Art, with offices in London, New York, Amsterdam, Frankfurt, and Sydney, recognized that a movement was beginning to evolve. "There was a move toward collage. With the CLC copying at £3.00 [c. US $5.00] a throw, a new direction was taking place. When you consider a basic set-up of computer, monitor, scanner, and printer was around £10,000 [c. US $16,000], it was hardly surprising that most illustrators stuck with the CLC for some time."

Meanwhile, alongside developments in digital technology, editorial design within the style press had started to evolve, taking on a more digital look. With the appointment of Neville Brody as Art Director at *The Face*, a bold new graphic language was developing. The introduction of the Mac sparked a revolution in publishing, with the ease of designing on-screen relegating paste-up design and production to the trash can. Within a few short years, the entire industry would be on board. For designers and art directors, increasingly aware of digital means of creation and reproduction, it was clear that those supplying the magazines with images would, at some point, have to fit into the digital loop.

The Impact of 128K RAM

Andy Martin left his job as Art Editor at *New Musical Express* to join the revolution. "I'd been laying out covers with pictures of cheesy mid-eighties bands and then quit in '85 as I could sense that something big was going to happen." Martin was introduced to the Mac a year before, by a key figure within Apple, when he was given a Mac with 128K of RAM to "play with, experiment with, and just see what I could do," he explains. "I was taken down to the PR office and was given the kit. It would have cost me an arm and a leg, and they just said 'take it.' How cool was that?" The impact on Martin's work was immense. He started to create digital illustrations for a variety of publications, all of which wanted to further their links with the changes in image creation that they knew were taking place.

With key figures like Wright and Martin in the UK, and John Hersey and J. Otto Seibold in the US making names for themselves by creating graphic images that went far beyond the boundaries of traditional illustration, others were starting to take notice. Publications willing to take risks with their visual approach gave new forms of image-making a platform, enabling other image-makers to follow their lead.

22. Paul Reilly, Topman/The Void, Kim Jones' collection launch
23. Miles Donovan, Tango/HHCL/*The Face* magazine cover, DeFace The Face
24. Jim Stoten, Gomez, *Silence* album sleeve

Profiles and Platforms

The most recent influx of digital image-making at *The Face* came when Graham Rounthwaite, having graduated with an MA in Illustration from the Royal College of Art in London, made the move from illustration image-making to design and art direction. Taking up the post of Art Editor at *The Face*, having worked on high-profile campaigns for Levi's as an illustrator in the late nineties, Rounthwaite began to make ripples. Despite enthusiasm for digital methods of working, it had taken almost a decade for a generation with the attitude and digital skills to match to emerge. Rounthwaite picked up on a small group of new image-makers, giving them creative freedom to produce innovative new work for the magazine. Jasper Goodall, Bump, and NEW were among this select group. It was through their work for *The Face* that offers of more lucrative projects for bigger clients rolled in.

The Death of the Style Press

The influence that the style press had enjoyed during its late-eighties heyday returned in the late nineties to make an impact on digital image-making and its relationship with other sectors of the design industry. The testing ground that *The Face* provided for new forms of working and the role that it played in bringing new talent to light is only now starting to gain the recognition and respect that it deserves. It may be a case of too little to late, however: *The Face* finally closed its doors in 2004, a year short of its twenty-fifth birthday.

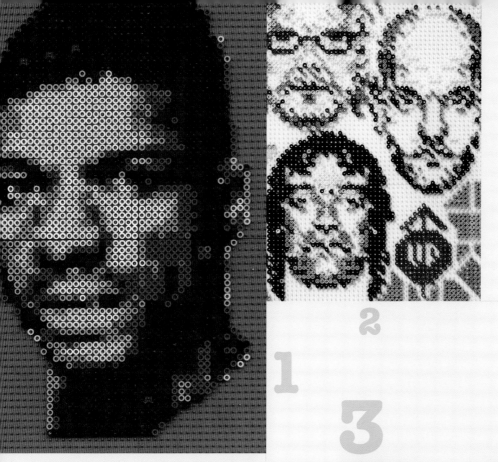

1
2
3

Ian Wright is the Daddy, maybe even the Granddaddy of contemporary illustration.

From Ian Wright's first job, at the end of the seventies, designing the cover of the Undertones' "Teenage Kicks" 7-inch single, to his frenetic weekly black-and-white portraits for *New Musical Express* in its eighties hey-day; from his in-your-face billboard campaign for Fosters Ice in the nineties, to his unique in-store installation for Issey Miyake in New York City in the noughties, Wright's work has spanned four decades. That is no small achievement.

Never one to stand still long enough to cash in on a creative approach, Wright has constantly forced his work into new directions. He has tested new developments in technology and mixed up techniques and materials, while creating unique visions that have remained in a constant flux.

Career Opportunities

Ian Wright never planned a career in illustration. Wright was working in a clerical job for the health service in Hoxton—before that part of East London was fashionable—when his colleagues, all women 30 years older, persuaded him to go to art school. A year of evening classes, another on an art and design foundation course, and three sharing a desk with Neville Brody at the London College of Printing, saw Wright enter the industry just as punk rock became new wave.

1. Personal project, Larry Levan
2. *Q* magazine, REM
3. Issey Miyake, Ghost Gorilla in progress

In May 1980, *The Face* launched its first-ever issue and Wright's work featured within. Featuring fashion, style, and music mixed together with contemporary design, *The Face* was the perfect outlet for Wright's fresh approach to image-making. His work, years later, bears very little resemblance to those early manic drawings, but the spirit within the work is still visible. Wright's use of materials has changed from job to job throughout his career. He has created images using just about anything that has come to hand. An early portrait of Grandmaster Flash saw Wright work entirely with salt to replicate cocaine as a reference to the seminal rap track "White Lines." Wright adopted photocopiers at an early stage, creating images by changing single color toners within the machine to mimic the screen-print process. He built layers of color from separate artworks into one final image. Working independently within Neville Brody's studio for many years, allowed Wright the luxury of dabbling with early Apple Macs. His choice of software in the early nineties was MacPaint, a funky little application created, as the name implies, for kids.

Portraits of the Artist
Portraits of Mike Tyson, Bjork, Ian Brown, Pete Townshend (the list goes on) for record sleeves and the music press, have allowed Wright to slip effortlessly between the analog and the digital. Wright is currently creating a portrait of civil rights campaigner Angela Davis, from 1,000 mascara brushes for *Black Book* magazine in the US. He is also creating a portrait of Henry Wellcome for The British Museum made entirely from reflective dots.

Wright commands huge respect for his leftfield approach to image-making, and it is not likely that his inventiveness will ever be tamed. Would-be illustrators and designers often approach Wright at his studio in East London for advice. Simple, he says: "Keep The Faith!"

4. Milliken carpets and rugs, Chief in progress
5. Milliken carpets and rugs, Chief
6. Howies, Junk Mail wardrobe
7. *New Musical Express* magazine, Grandmaster Flash
8. Personal project, Jean-Michel Basquiat
9. *Esquire* magazine, Mike Tyson

1

Profile:
Michael Gillette

California dreaming: this image-maker goes from "acoustic" painting to making digital pop art in the sun.

California's year-round sunshine should be the ideal place to grow outdoors—after all, the state's symbols include the giant redwood tree and the golden poppy. Michael Gillette's studio faces out on his small back yard, wooden decked and adorned with potted plants that, he admits "need some help." Gardening is not Gillette's thing.

Untitled
Making images, however, is. From the moment he won a book token as first prize in a school art competition—for his first major piece, *Untitled*—he was hooked. "From then on, it was the only road for me," he explains. "Well, I did want to join The Beatles, but that gig was long gone." Gillette admits to more than a passing interest in music. Two weeks out of college, in 1992, he won his first commission for the band St. Etienne, creating portraits of the group's members. This exposure saw Gillette pick up regular work for monthly music magazine *Select*, in London. His first job was to create images for a piece that ushered in Britpop. Over the next six years, while he was

3

1. Birth of Dub, personal project
2. The Five Boroughs, The Beastie Boys, Web site
3. Stereowolf, T-Shirt

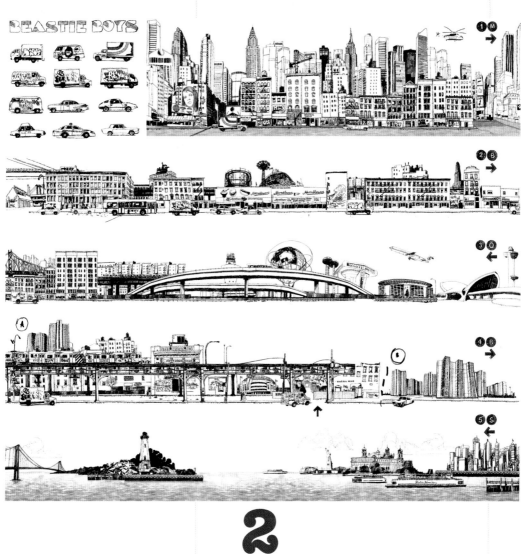

4. Oil War, T-Shirt
5. Black Bear Creek, T-Shirt
6. King Mo Dirtbags, T-Shirt

based in London, Gillette worked on numerous projects and commissions that included diversions into pop promos for Britpop band Elastica.

While watching paint dry in 1999, Gillette decided that "it was time to embrace the digital revolution." Exhibiting his last "acoustic" works in Soho's trendy watering hole The Groucho Club was a landmark in his career. Gillette soon realized that being digital meant he could be almost anywhere on the planet. His decision to up and leave London for San Francisco in 2002 was inspired by a trip to the city back in 1997. "It's a truly unique place, small enough to be intimate with, but big enough to warrant a truly gigantic record store," explains Gillette, quickly referencing the city back to his love of music. "It's on the coast, the weather is great, and it's foxy pretty."

Inspirations

Reflecting on the artists and designers who have inspired his work, Gillette admits that music, not surprisingly, has played a huge part. "I'm obviously a big pop art fan, possibly because it was so connected to music," he states. He is also a fan of New York–based Pushpin Studios, whose work by founders Seymour Chwast and Milton Glaser made a phenomenal impact on design from the fifties though to the eighties. "Those Pushpin folk could draw like God," he states. "The most recent artist whose work really made me want to weep is Roger Andersson." Andersson, a Swedish watercolor artist, published a book of paintings in 2004—*Letters from Mayhem*. The simplicity and beauty of his work echoes Gillette's curve-ball take on popular culture.

Organic Processes

Gillette's projects start in a simple manner. "I read the brief, mull it over, and think up an idea, research it, look stuff up on the Internet, draw/paint the elements I think I need, scan them, and start fiddling around" is his honest description of his working process. "Generally, during this process, I decide on a better idea and redraw elements to fit," he explains. "It's quite organic." Gillette's gardening skills can't be described in the same way...

7. Tommy Shots, *Young Heart Attack* sleeve design
8. Ban Criminally Logged Timber, Greenpeace poster

1. *Surface* magazine, Adobe Software promotion
2. Big Active, Gogo digital print

Dark, moody, raw, and sexual best describe Jasper Goodall's influences and subject matter.

"A mag from Japan called *Tattoo Burst*, a book of erotic Chinese art, an incredible Korean book that categorizes thousands of animals and gives 50 different stylized representations of each of them …" Jasper Goodall is describing his desk top in his studio. He continues, "… loads of empty tea and coffee cups, bills I haven't paid, bits of paper with my drawings on them, and, oh yes, all my computer shit."

The fact that Goodall's choice of kit, including a high-end Mac running Photoshop and FreeHand, a Wacom tablet, scanner, and all manner of digital devices, seems to excite him far less than his felt-tips, pop-a-point pencils, crayons, and his wealth of global visual reference materials is an indication of how this image-maker approaches his creative work.

Creative Control

Goodall draws upon a range of interests, including a sojourn in Japan for training in martial arts. He has become pretty adept at creating fashion-based but gutsy images as part of major advertising campaigns for a range of clients, including Levi's and Nike. It is, however, his work for defunct style magazine *The Face* that always excited him most, as creative control remained firmly within his own grasp. "I hate clients who dictate. I once worked on a very big project for a stressed art director who slammed the phone down on me, so we only communicated via e-mail. One e-mail, demanding changes to my artwork, angered me so much that I spat at his message on my screen!"

Angry Young Man

Goodall is obviously prepared to stand by his principles; he once attacked a UK national newspaper, *The Observer*, for making changes to one of his images, removing a semierect penis without his permission. Leading monthly design publication *Creative Review* ran a two-page feature on the fiasco, looking in depth at issues of digital manipulation and ownership of copyright after Goodall made them aware of his treatment at the hands of the newspaper. "The best thing about working as a freelance illustrator must be the freedom," explains Goodall, "but the worst thing has to be the number of talentless art directors who desire control!"

Dark and Dirty

Sex remains at the forefront of the subject matter explored within Goodall's work. He cites pornography, along with eighties' singer Gary Numan and US author Bret Easton Ellis, as influences. This goes some way to explaining his visual take on the subject. His images are littered with fashionable and beautiful, sometimes vacant, other times powerful-looking women, with an undercurrent of a much darker, moodier place. It seems fitting that Goodall has just completed another fashion range; his second line of bikinis, the first in conjunction with his agent, Big Active, launched at a fashionable gallery in West London. Goodall's 2-D digital fashion world meets the real world in 3-D form, harnessing the same snarly attitude as that captured within his illustrations.

3. Personal project, Crows
4. Bikini range, Jolly Roger
5. *The Face* magazine, Commune

2

Mixing Media & Techniques

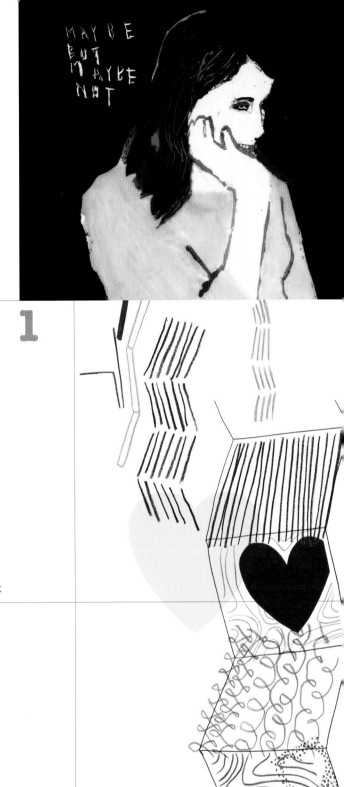

Risk-taking and an appreciation of accidental mistakes, combined with a solid underpinning in the language of creativity, leads to new forms of image-making.

In 1973, Luke Rhinehart wrote and published a novel that has remained a permanent fixture in student apartments throughout the US and Europe. *The Dice Man* is the story of a psychiatrist, locked into a life of order and routine, who decides to let the roll of the dice govern his every decision. This intriguing story captured, and continues to capture, the imagination of a youth yet to fully comprehend how to live their lives, how to navigate and negotiate the complexities of day-to-day living. More importantly, as well as appearing to offer an alternative route through the mainstream and mundane existence led by the majority of the population, the book forced a view of risk-taking and chance as a glamorous and exciting lifestyle choice. Despite rarely appearing on book lists for art and design students—most art schools opt for books on theory and practice rather than literature—the attitude and mindset of the novel impresses those with an artistic and creative viewpoint: the importance of risk-taking within creative image-making has so often been overlooked.

Perfect Platforms
Ensuring that the conditions within art and design education are conducive to taking creative risks is just part of the problem that has faced art schools for many years. While design education recognizes the benefits of making and learning from mistakes, of being unfazed by traversing new routes in order to produce exciting and challenging visual solutions, it is often criticized for being too unaware of commercial realities and constraints. Creating a perfect platform, available at the right price, and accessible to the right number of students, has never been a simple task. The modern-day "solution" owes much to an approach that was born in Germany early in the twentieth century.

1. Ceri Amphlett, personal project, Maybe
2. Jenny Bowers, Penguin Books, catalog introduction
3. Supergympie, *Studio* magazine, Killer Technique
4. Mr. Bingo, personal project, I Had Sex With My Own Ass In Front Of My Dog
5. Andy Martin, Department for International Development, The Granary

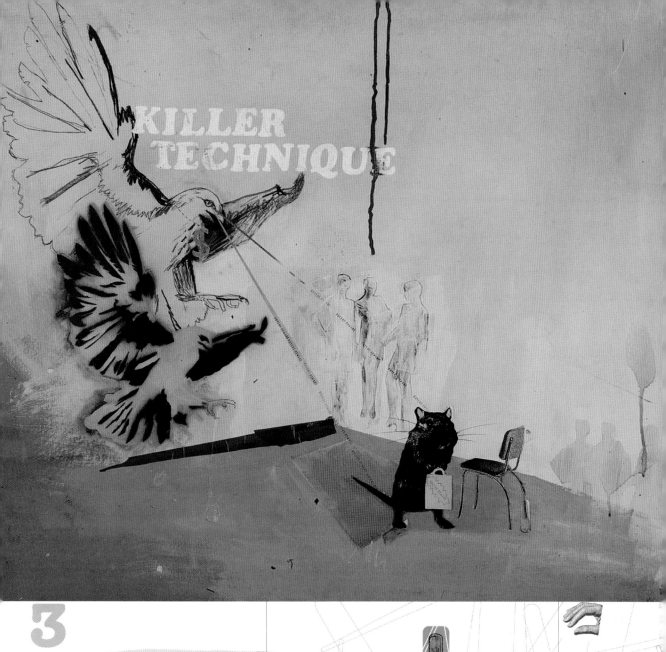

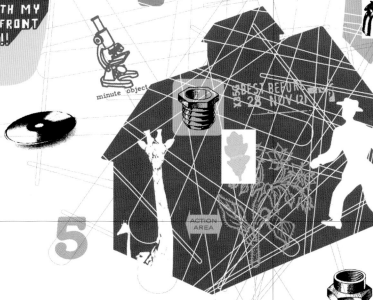

9

Building House

The Bauhaus design school was founded in Weimar in 1919. Although initially concerned with the teaching of architecture (Bauhaus is German for "building house"), it attempted to create a new unison between art and industry. The Bauhaus approach revolutionized the teaching of art and design, and its influence can still be felt throughout Europe, the US, and even Japan. Underpinning the Bauhaus ethos was the fact that artists, designers, and craftspeople worked together to create the removal of conventional subject barriers. Students studied a variety of disciplines, with initial lecture-based study followed by hands-on training in workshops. Subjects included the study of nature, fabrics, materials and tools, geometry, color and composition, and construction and presentation. Students undertook classes across a range of disciplines including drawing, painting, sculpture, photography, typography, advertising, furniture design, and interior design. Through the teachings of such eminent artists and designers as Johannes Itten, Walter Gropius, Herbert Bayer, Wassily Kandinsky, Laszlo Moholy-Nagy, and Paul Klee, students of the Bauhaus school were taught, in the words of its manifesto, "the only thing that can be learned; the language of creativity." The mix and marriage of materials that this encouraged, together with the breaking down of boundaries between artists and craftspeople, produced a unique foundation stone for today's education of the artist/designer.

Shock of the New

Nearly a century after the introduction of this Bauhaus method of art education, and several decades on from the risk-taking proposals put forward by Rhinehart in *The Dice Man*, it would appear that these two seemingly unassociated events have both played a part in the development of recent movements in creative image-making. It is the mix of media and materials, along with the element of surprise and risk, that motivates many of the people working in digital image-making today.

In the mid-seventies, a documentary series on modern art, and its accompanying book, used the title "The Shock of the New." This reflected the view of modern art held by the general public at the time,

and fitted the program brilliantly. It is also an apt description of the effect that digital technology had on the fairly safe and secure world of illustration when it was unleashed toward the end of the following decade. While the forward-thinking, fashion-conscious graphic design world grappled with digital technology from the earliest opportunity, illustration kept much of the hardware, software, and new working methods at arm's length. The humble illustrator wanted nothing to do with the digital, preferring older, traditional, and more established ways of working. Unlike the innovative Bauhaus approach to materials and methods, most illustrators followed entrenched practices; it took some time for digital technology to break into and change their working methodology.

10

11

12

13

11. Andrew Rae, personal project, *Perverted Science*
12. Tim Marrs, Orion Books, *City Primeval*
13. Billie Jean, Parker Pens/Pentagram, Ballpoint Fiftieth Anniversary
14. Tatsuro Kiuchi, Tokyo Illustrators' Society, Red Shoes
15. Lee Ford, *Big Issue* magazine, Angel Resendez: America's Prolific Killer

"New Technology"

On reflection, it is clear that the illustrator/image-makers' preoccupation with and love for traditional methods has played a huge part in the recent combination of tried and tested techniques with digital technology. "New" technology once meant digital technology, but as more and more art students grow up with access to computers, this description is no longer appropriate. For many of these students, the "traditional" techniques and methods could more accurately be described as "new."

Old-School Art

Art and design education, at its best, still introduces students to many forms of artistic expression through a range of disciplines that includes etching, lithography, and screen printing; black-and-white photography and darkroom processing; analog animation; and bookbinding, letterpress, and woodblock printing. Students learn how to improve their drawing skills through observational and interpretative drawing in the studio and life class; they are taught theories and principles of color, layout, type, and image; and are given a full grounding in the history of their discipline. The combination of this practical, theoretical, and cultural underpinning of the subject with digital technology has opened up a range of working methods that are defining a new visual esthetic. The super-realistic, close-to-perfection results that first appeared when image-editing applications, such as Photoshop, were launched, and the clean-edge, mechanical drawing techniques employed by users of Illustrator and FreeHand have started to fade into the background as a more "messed-up" esthetic has emerged.

Graduates often discover that recreating the art school studio is an expensive endeavor, but financial requirements do shrink annually. The normal host of input devices has not varied dramatically from year to year—the mouse, keyboard, and scanner have been around a while, and other devices have become less expensive. Graphics tablets, digital cameras, and digital camcorders are all cases in point. Much of the most interesting work being created today utilizes older techniques within modern technology to create genuinely new working practices.

14

15

Make Mistakes

The casual mistake of misregistration, the overprint of one color, the odd bleed of another, the drip of a paint mixed a little too wet, or the slight sticking of ink in the mesh of a silk screen are all accidents that may take a visual image in a new direction. It is often the case that "things going wrong" can dictate new directions in work; recreating these accidents using digital means, although entirely possible, requires firsthand experience of working with traditional materials and methods. Composing an image of painterly textures, creating layers using hand-drawn elements, adding swirls and swishes of real-time and real-life color can imbue it with a timeless depth.

The journey through education and practice into creating a unique and personal visual language or working style is a complex one. Staying ahead of the game, constantly mixing techniques and creating new working methods to keep one step ahead of the copyists is never an easy task, but experimentation with materials, risk-taking, and stepping into the unknown provides the most conducive environment for change and for new work to be created.

16. Ceri Amphlett, Parker Pens/Pentagram, Ballpoint Fiftieth Anniversary
17. Chrissie Macdonald, self-published book, *Woodland*
18. Lee Ford, personal project, Too Many Cooks ...

19

20

I'M NO GOOD

2

1

Dubious drawings, impending gloom, and bits of flotsam—a desktop in East London.

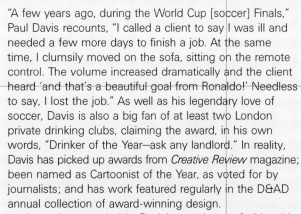

3

FAKE LONDON GENIUS

"A few years ago, during the World Cup [soccer] Finals," Paul Davis recounts, "I called a client to say I was ill and needed a few more days to finish a job. At the same time, I clumsily moved on the sofa, sitting on the remote control. The volume increased dramatically and the client heard 'and that's a beautiful goal from Ronaldo!' Needless to say, I lost the job." As well as his legendary love of soccer, Davis is also a big fan of at least two London private drinking clubs, claiming the award, in his own words, "Drinker of the Year—ask any landlord." In reality, Davis has picked up awards from *Creative Review* magazine; been named as Cartoonist of the Year, as voted for by journalists; and has work featured regularly in the D&AD annual collection of award-winning design.

Instantly recognizable, Davis' wry takes on fashionable East London types have been spotted across the pages of various magazines and newspapers, including *Dazed and Confused*, *Time Out*, and *The Independent*. In fact, it is an eight-page fashion feature for *The Independent on Sunday* magazine, commissioned by Art Director Jo Dale in 1997, that Davis attributes to being a career-defining moment. "The phone hasn't stopped ringing since that job, thanks to Jo," says Davis.

1. I'm No Good, personal project
2. I'm Brilliant, personal project
3. FAKE London Genius poster

A WORK OF EVIL

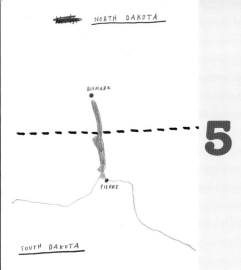

NORTH DAKOTA

BISMARK

5

PIERRE

SOUTH DAKOTA

4

Paris, Tokyo, Stockholm, New York

Recently, that phone has also rung from clients all around the globe. "I've worked on a cookbook for a Canadian publisher, a series of images for an exhibition in Paris, a set of prints for a gallery in Tokyo, and a calendar for Save The Children in Stockholm," Davis casually admits. He has also had a couple of books published recently, including one of his unpublished work and another on how Americans and Britons view each other. Davis toured the US researching, drawing, and speaking to people as he traveled, recording their thoughts and opinions.

Digital Documentation

Davis has adopted digital technology purely as a means to document, archive, market, and distribute his work. When describing his working environment, he says very little about his choice of hardware. In fact, he dryly lists the following items as taking pride of place on his desk: "a computer, a cup of tea, a pile of papers I'm too scared to look at, external hard drive, bits of flotsam, scanner, dubious drawings, impending gloom, video camera, mouse, dodgy erotica." The surface of the desk may describe more the Davis state of mind than any working process.

Capturing the Moment

Many of Davis' drawings are done on the move. He works in small sketchbooks, capturing conversations, moments, and moods which are then translated into final pieces back in his studio. Quick sketches, doodles, drawings, and observations are a vital part of the Davis working method. He once exhibited 3,000 drawings on Post-its at the Dazed and Confused Gallery in London. Davis' continued hard work and determination have paid off. He has come a very long way since his first commission for the long-dead listings magazine *City Limits*; "I got paid 12 quid. Honest!" The Paul Davis World Cup "honesty" springs to mind once again.

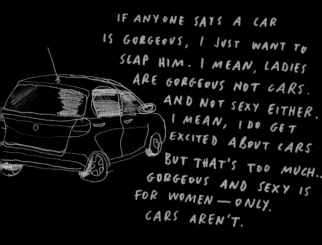

IF ANYONE SAYS A CAR
IS GORGEOUS, I JUST WANT TO
SLAP HIM. I MEAN, LADIES
ARE GORGEOUS NOT CARS.
AND NOT SEXY EITHER.
I MEAN, I DO GET
EXCITED ABOUT CARS
BUT THAT'S TOO MUCH..
GORGEOUS AND SEXY IS
FOR WOMEN — ONLY.
CARS AREN'T.

6

CECI N'EST PAS
MICROSOFT

DAVIS

7

8

FAKE
LONDON
GENIUS

9

10

FAKE
LONDON
GENIUS

FUTURENET +33 0289 900 192
FOURWORKS +44 20 7251 6180

11

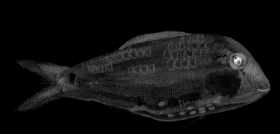

JUBILANT

12

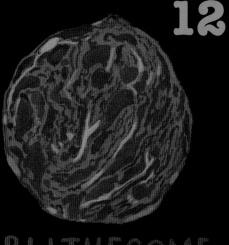

BLITHESOME

13

吉本新喜劇
N¥C ロンドン
88

DAVIS

14

Profile: Marion Deuchars

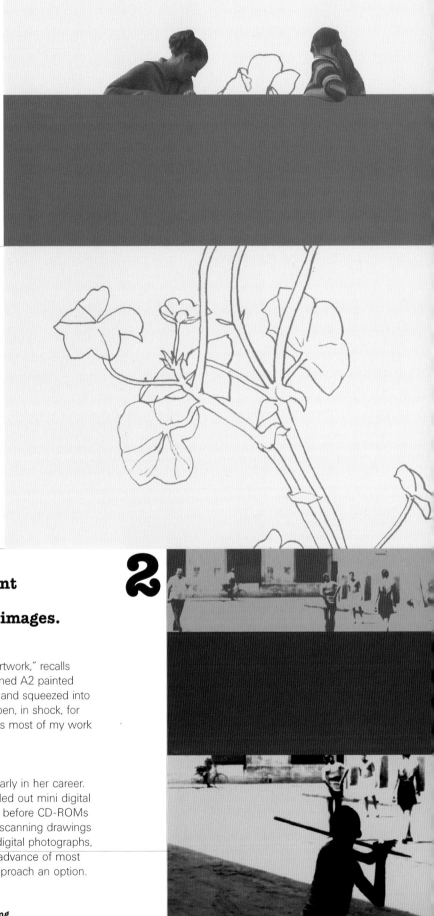

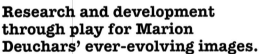

Research and development through play for Marion Deuchars' ever-evolving images.

"I have numerous incidents of missing artwork," recalls Marion Deuchars. "The best was a returned A2 painted illustration, folded carefully into quarters and squeezed into an A4 envelope. My mouth remained open, in shock, for some time afterwards. Luckily, nowadays most of my work is sent digitally."

Learning to Love the Digital

Deuchars learnt to love the computer early in her career. Prior to agency representation, she mailed out mini digital portfolios saved onto floppy disks, long before CD-ROMs were affordable. Work that began from scanning drawings and paintings, and later combined her digital photographs, presented well as a digital portfolio, in advance of most image-makers even considering this approach an option.

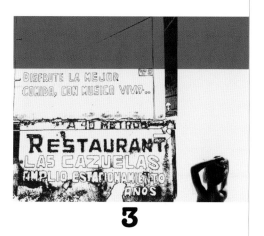

4

3

Computer, Desk, and Play Desk

Deuchars is one of a rare breed of image-makers who continue to adapt and push their work into new directions. It is her studio setup that enables this continued research and development. "I have two desks, one for the computer and one for playing on," she explains. "On the computer desk right now there is a G4, a Wacom tablet, a calculator, a Nikon Coolpix, a telephone, a diary, and a list of things to do." Deuchars makes an attempt to define the other desk. "My play desk is full of stuff; paints, paper, three large tubs of brushes in water (that have been there too long), four different plastic palettes, six different rolls of tape, tubes of gouache, a box of charcoal, various boxes of stencils … That's all I can see on the 'top layer' right now."

Working in illustration since graduating from the Royal College of Art, London, at the end of the eighties, Deuchars now teaches there and can count numerous working illustrators and image-makers as former students of hers.

Deuchars believes that getting out and meeting clients is the best way to generate commissions when first starting out. "Agents are not a good idea at first. It is important to 'pound the boards' and meet and understand one's own industry personally," she explains. "Some of my original contacts are people I still work with and have a good relationship with."

Bonus

Deuchars has picked up a Creative Futures Award, membership of the prestigious Alliance Graphique International (AGI), and an enviable client list. Deuchars is in demand. Her current ongoing projects include three book jacket designs, a chair design for a company in Helsinki, color studies for the Cricket Building in Derby, England, and 15 portraits for *Wallpaper** magazine. She would have it no other way. "I like making images; being paid for it is a bonus."

5

1. Untitled, Planeta catalog image
2. Baseball, personal project
3. Les Cazuelas, Spain, personal project
4. Picture This, British Council poster
5. Cuba, personal project

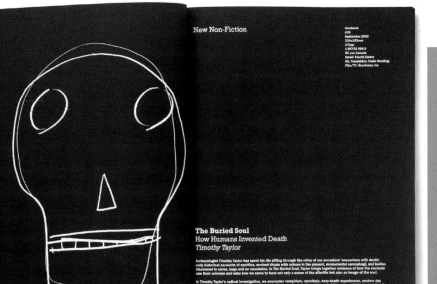

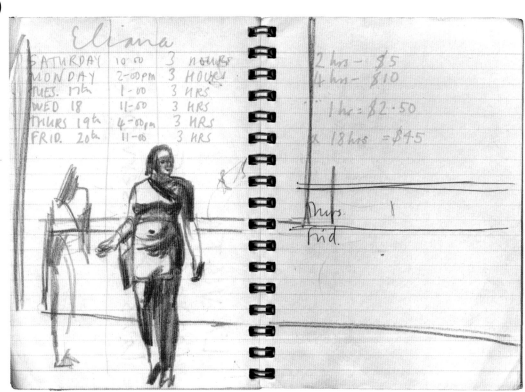

6. Untitled, 4th Estate catalog image
7. *Las palabras*, book jacket
8. Untitled sketchbook image, personal project

2

1

3

IT specialist required for busy ex-print-maker...

"In my precomputer days I worked using relief printing, a very long-winded process that often meant all-night sessions in the studio to meet deadlines," explains Shonagh Rae who shares Studio 100 with around 20 designers, architects, and other illustrators. "Occasionally," she elaborates, "I would have to courier work that was still drying. One time when I got a copy of the magazine that an illustration appeared in, I realized that the artwork had completely stuck to the inside of the envelope in transit. The art director had made a vague attempt at peeling it off, but it had gone to print anyway! I booked to go on a Photoshop course the next day."

Image-maker and IT specialist

That early lesson was a tough one, but it changed the course of Rae's work in a way she could not have imagined. Currently one of the busiest image-makers in the editorial and publishing fields, Rae has successfully developed her time-consuming, labor-intensive print techniques into a digital process that echoes her earlier work, evoking much of its texture and richness, while never needing hours to dry. For Rae, though, the digital comes with another set of problems. "One of the worst things about what I do is having to be my own IT specialist," she explains.

1. *Deadly Kin* book jacket
2. Euryanthe, *The Independent* newspaper, short story
3. Juice Detox, *The Independent* newspaper, feature

4

4. Crimea, *Highlife Magazine*, feature
5. *Powder Monkey* book jacket
6. Genetic Sexual Attraction, *The Guardian* newspaper, article
7. London Wine Fair, *Highlife Magazine*, feature

The fact that Rae is currently working on numerous projects means that she may well be on the way to employing her own IT professional. "I'm working on a piece for *MAMM* magazine—an American publication for women suffering from breast cancer—three book jackets for novelist Jake Arnott, another for a new author, Louise Dean, images for *New Scientist* magazine, others for an annual company report, and some editorial stuff," lists Rae. Represented by the leading contemporary illustration agency Heart, Rae understands the value of having an agent to assist in managing the financial aspects of the job. "I decided to work through an agent as, like a lot of flimsy illustrators, I don't like the messy business of talking money."

Personal Vision

Rae is very happy with her current studio setup, but the route to joining Studio 100 was not straightforward. "My first studio was above Burger King in Camden Town, and in the years since it seems like I have shared a studio with pretty much every illustrator and image-maker in London," she explains. Rae's approach to her work, her journey from print studio to computer screen via numerous studios, is echoed in the advice she gives to those just starting out. "Develop a personal way of working and then decide where you might fit into illustration, rather than the other way around." The IT skills can be picked up on the way.

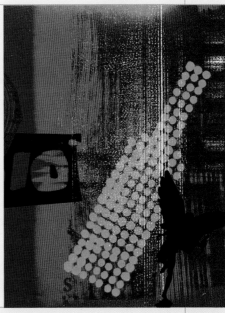

Revival, Appropriation, and Reuse

3

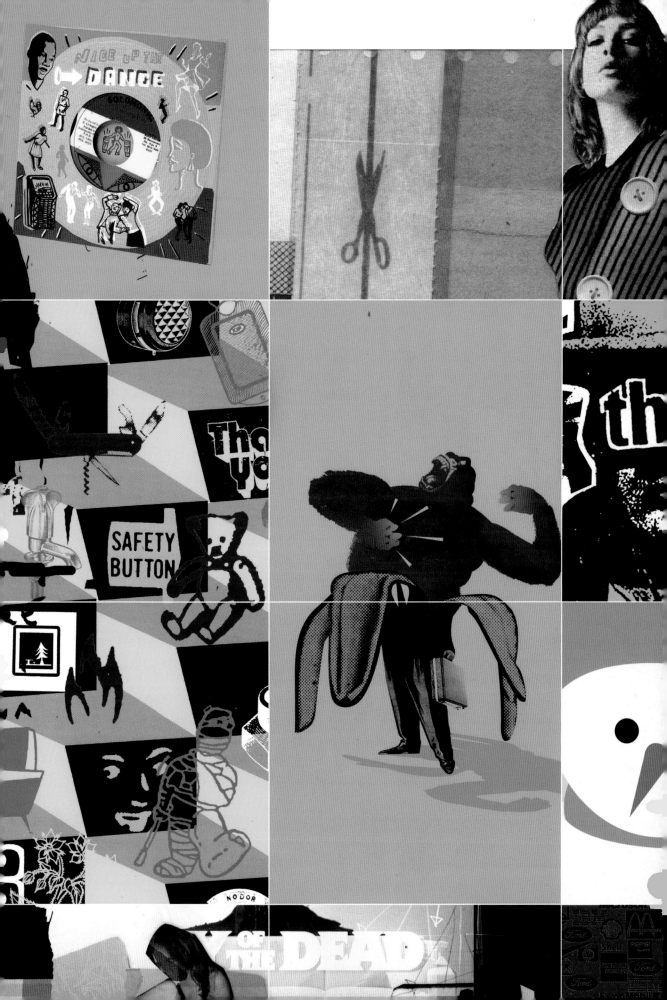

"Computers are to design as microwaves are to cooking," exclaimed legendary US graphic designer Milton Glaser.

At the time he made that comment, Glaser had a valid point. With the introduction of digital technology, much of the graphic design being created was essentially a reheated, re-served version of what had been made earlier, using traditional methods. Although there were a number of key individuals pushing the technology and creating entirely new ways of working—namely April Greiman in graphic design and John Hersey in illustration, both in the US—most of the work did not break any boundaries. Glaser, a prolific designer and illustrator, made his name with witty conceptual design solutions as part of Pushpin Studios in New York, which he cofounded with Seymour Chwast, in 1954. It was Glaser's concept-led approach to visual communication, rather than the traditional esthetic style, that ignited a new vision of graphic design at that time.

I ♥ Logos

When he designed the I♥NY logo for the New York State Department of Commerce in 1976, Glaser could not have foreseen just how much impact one piece of graphic design could have. Widely regarded as the most imitated design in the history of the logo, today it can be found anywhere and everywhere. From coffee cup to T-shirt, from bumper sticker to baseball cap, the logo has been reused and reinterpreted, and the idea reappropriated for all manner of uses. Most versions are a pale imitation of Glaser's logo, and while often claimed the sincerest form of flattery, imitation in this case has lessened and cheapened the impact of the original.

The simplicity of the design is the perfect mix of type and image. The heart symbol demonstrates the perfect use of an existing icon, typifying image-making based on the reuse of existing images, symbols, and signs—a mix-and-match approach that steadily gained momentum as it became technically easier and culturally more accepted.

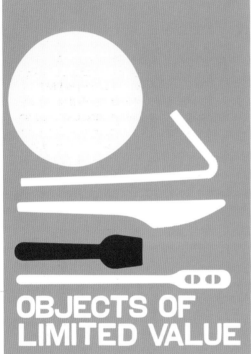

5. Mr. Bingo, Oxfam, Children Are Born With These Arms
6. Anthony Burrill, personal project, Objects of Limited Value
7. Brian Cairns, Ridley Scott Associates Films, Jake Scott wedding invitation
8. David Foldvari, Stoique (Japan), Graffiti Meets Windows (live painting event)
9. Martin O'Neill, *Adweek* magazine, Modest Change
10. Faile, Pro-Ked, sneaker design

9

10

Digital Revolution
In 1975, the first computer to warrant serious attention—the MITS (Micro Instrumentation Telemetry Systems) Altair—went on sale. It required assembly and needed expansion cards to run the keyboard and monitor. Two thousand were sold at US $439 (c. £240) each. The following year, Apple made its debut with the Apple II, the first model being a short-lived experimental precursor. Unveiled at the first West Coast Computer Fair in San Francisco, Apple II boasted a built-in keyboard, an audiocassette drive for storage, and just 4KB of RAM. The Apple II retailed at US $1,298 (c. £700). The Commodore Pet was also launched in 1976, but perhaps bigger news, although not at the time, was the setting up of Microsoft in Albuquerque, New Mexico, by Bill Gates and Paul Allen. The digital revolution had begun, though it was yet to play a part in graphic design.

Model 914
One of the first pieces of equipment to play a role in defining the reuse of images was the humble office photocopier. Invented by Chester F. Carlson in 1937 and patented as Electric Photography in the US in 1942, it took a further 18 years to find a business that was interested in the technology. Finally, the Haloid Company brought Carlson's idea to market. A year after its successful launch of the first ever fully automated photocopier, the company changed its name to Xerox Corporation. Model 914 was named after the paper size it could handle—9 x 14in.

With the photocopier starting to make an appearance in offices during the sixties and, as prices came down, appearing in design companies, copy shops, and public libraries throughout the seventies, the ability to create inexpensive, technically straightforward, and graphically accurate copies proved a real asset for freelance designers and image-makers. No longer were expensive PMT (photomechanical transfer) machines needed to create black-and-white copies of original artwork: a one-person design/illustration company could produce similar results with a cheap photocopier. This new ease in reproduction led to a proliferation of graphics that reused existing images.

Cut-and-Paste
Cultural factors also played a part. In the mid-seventies, punk rock had a dramatic impact on graphic design. In New York, emerging through the clubs, it manifested itself predominantly through music, while in the UK the focus was broader, with music, fashion, graphics, and design all feeling its influence. The speed-fueled sound of punk required a graphic language that depicted a new raw energy as far removed visually as it was aurally from what came before. The do-it-yourself concept of punk was translated through the work of graphic artists and designers like Jamie Reid, for the Sex Pistols, and Malcolm Garrett, for the Buzzcocks.

DINERO

11

13

14

Jamie Reid created the ransom-note, cut-and-paste graphic language that later defined the look and feel of punk while he was designing *Suburban Press*, a radical political magazine that ran for five years from 1970. He created a range of subversive graphics and slogans that were printed onto stickers. These included "Save Petrol— Burn Cars" and "Keep Warm This Winter—Make Trouble." The use of cheap materials, the photocopier, black-and-white imagery, and ripped edges came to characterize punk. Malcolm McLaren, manager of the Sex Pistols, invited Reid to design graphics for the band while he and Vivienne Westwood created their own avenue for punk rebellion through the clothes they designed for their shop, Sex. T-shirts depicted cut-up swastikas, pornographic images, and Union Jacks in tatters. In true punk style, Reid reappropriated a portrait of the Queen, by Cecil Beaton, for the Sex Pistols' single "God Save the Queen." The Queen's portrait also appeared on T-shirts, with a safety pin piercing her lips. Reusing, reconfiguring, and reinterpreting, long before recycling became the norm, punk led a revolution in redefining the visuals of graphic design.

15

16

17

From Punk to Hip-Hop

When rap music emerged from the New York housing projects in the late seventies, it introduced the culture of reusing beats and sounds from existing records. One of the first rap recordings, "Rapper's Delight" by the Sugarhill Gang, was released in 1979. It utilized bass lines and beats from the disco track "Good Times," originally recorded by Chic. "Rapper's Delight" went on to become the biggest-selling 12-inch single in history, shifting more than two million copies around the globe and adding a word to the popular vocabulary—hip-hop is a lyric used in the song. Rap borrowed from gospel and jazz, soul, funk, and disco, and its characteristic remixing of beats from different sources became known as sampling. Associations and links between punk and hip-hop have often been commented on. Don Letts, a filmmaker and former punk DJ, recalls that "punk was a complete subculture. Nothing since then has been so complete. I still live by all that shit. Hip-hop is black punk rock."

Visual Sampling

Reusing images, icons, signs, and symbols has been part of image-making and graphic art for many years. As punk stole from the establishment and hip-hop sampled from existing musical genres, so Andy Warhol and pop art before them plundered popular visual culture. Marilyn Monroe, Campbell's soup cans, and Coca-Cola bottles were all up for grabs. Digital technology was not the instigator, but it has made aspects of the process easier; getting access to a cheap scanner to import "found" elements into a design is now a far simpler process than gaining access to a PMT camera or a photocopier was over 20 years ago.

Shifts in expectations, led by changes in how both music and design can be created, have given the visualizer a new creative freedom. Access to images has never been greater, whether through a 30-second Google image search or wandering around a flea market or garage sale picking up printed ephemera. There is always an image crying out to be reused and given new life.

18. Joe Magee, *New Scientist* magazine, DNA Palm Reading
19. Richard May, The Apartment, Under Construction party invite
20. NEW, *Time Out* magazine, The Money Trap: Criminal Cons with Student Loans

1

OBJECTS OF
LIMITED VALUE

2

SITOI
KITU!

UMOJA
NI NGUVU

IF YOU SUSPECT ANY CORRUPTION PLEASE REPORT IT TO US AT:
KENYA ANTI-CORRUPTION COMMISSION
INTEGRITY CENTRE, MILIMANI / VALLEY RD. JUNCTION,
PO BOX 61130 NAIROBI
TEL: 2718812 / 2719553 FAX: 2719757 e-mail: kacc@integrity.go.ke

1. *Objects of Limited Value*, personal project, limited-edition book
2. Sitoi Kitu!, Kenyan Anti-Corruption Commission, poster

Engaging and amusing his audience are prime motives for this globe-trotting image-maker.

Travel plays a part in Anthony Burrill's search for inspiration. He enjoys the experience. "Seeing different places is exciting." The way things look and smell differently, he says, is what can effect changes in his work, "although it's not until you get back home that you can start to process all the new things you've seen. Then it starts to seep into the work quite subconsciously."

Enthusiast at Work

Burrill's work is quiet and unassuming, but has a presence and sense of humor that engages the viewer. "I'm very interested in things and I love finding out about new things," he states. "I like meeting new people and seeing how they approach their work. I think my work has a friendliness that engages with people. I don't load my work with layers of meaning—it's bright and cheerful. It's an extension of me. It's very simple too, like me."

3

WORK
HARD
&
BE NICE
TO PEOPLE

4

5

Anthony Burrill 2004   www.anthonyburrill.com   Printed by Adams of Rye

Engage and Amuse

There is a refreshing honesty to Burrill's frank admission
of how his work communicates. There is nothing cool or
ironic in his descriptions of the process; what you see is
what you get. "I use lots of little phrases that I pick up
in conversation. 'Work hard and be nice to people' was
overheard at the checkout in a supermarket. As soon
as I heard it, I saw it as a poster. It made itself, really,"
he admits. "Whatever medium I'm working in, the basic
function is the same—to engage and amuse other people,"
he states.

Burrill's approach to image-making has won him many
admirers, and he is in constant demand. It is his work for
award-winning Dutch advertising agency KesselsKramer
that he regards most highly, however. "The first time
I worked for them was for the Hans Brinker budget hotel.
That was my first 'big break.' Subsequently, I've worked
on a couple of campaigns for Diesel with them," he recalls.
"It's always great because they give me so much freedom.
The results are always very pure and stand out from
everything else."

Combining Processes

Working for print and screen both appeal to Burrill.
Recent projects include creating Web sites for two of his
favorite bands, Kraftwerk and Air. However, it is his love
for a range of working methods that motivates and
informs his work. "I'm interested in combining processes—
drawings scanned in, then colored on the computer—or
finding old techniques—photocopying and letterpress
printing are still my favorites," he adds. "I always have a
digital camera with me to record things, funny bits of type,
or interesting buildings. I use the photos as starting points
for drawings." He has yet to find a button on his camera
that records a "smell," though.

Last year alcohol
contributed to 3 deaths
and 349 injuries.

CAUTION. PLEASE BE CAREFUL AFTER A FEW DRINKS.

UNDERGROUND

3. Sock Kid, Sony PlayStation, character development
4. Work Hard & Be Nice to People, personal project, poster
5. London Underground, public service poster
6. *Magic Land*, personal project, limited-edition book

6

OREST WITH CLOUD

Profile: Brett Ryder

Staring at album sleeves and painting motorcycle jackets was the inspiration for Brett Ryder.

Brett Ryder admits that getting a computer was a career-defining moment after his graduation from the Illustration Master of Arts program at Central St Martins College in London in 1994. His eclectic approach to image-making—he uses a combination of found images and ephemera collaged together with his own drawings—made the transition to digital an interesting one. Ryder has a fervent interest in old motorcycles, and rebuilds the manifold on his BSA 650 with a dexterity that translates well to his use of Photoshop to "build" his images.

"I did loads of stuff as a kid," offers Ryder about his route into image-making and illustration. "I was the one everyone came to when they wanted their favorite album or band painted on their leather jacket. I even had my own airbrush. We did have some strange characters turning up on our doorstep, though." Linked to that early career move, Ryder talks a little about his dream project. "I've always dreamed of doing the Rolling Stones tour stuff, stage props, animations for their videos, T-shirts, the whole deal."

1. *The Observer* newspaper, Satisfaction
2. *The Observer* newspaper, Hot Weather

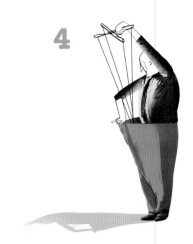

Rock 'n' Roll

Music has always featured highly in Ryder's life. "Staring at album sleeves was once a full-time occupation," he admits, insisting that the once-stylish Roxy Music are his all-time favorite band. But he claims that finding "socks with no holes or, if lucky, a pair" is the right start to a creative day. Working from a studio at home, Ryder's sartorial elegance is no match for that of his hero Bryan Ferry. "I can sit around all day in my pyjamas, and nobody is any the wiser," he explains, in a manner that could best be described as tongue-in-cheek.

"It is all I Know"

Ryder's work is cheeky. It retains a playful quirkiness, first developed in his early student pieces, and combines the real with the unreal, the literal with the imaginary. Ryder's illustrations regularly greet readers of the UK's daily broadsheets—*The Guardian*, *The Independent*, and *The Times*—as well as *The Observer* on Sundays. It is, perhaps, the surreal nature of Ryder's images that works so well with the journalism published by the cream of the UK's newspaper industry.

Despite the constant flow of work, which includes projects for BP, NatWest Bank, and Penguin Books, Ryder worries about his fate. "The best thing about working as an illustrator is that it is all I've wanted to do and it is all I know," he states. "The worst thing about being in illustration is knowing it is all I know."

3. *The Guardian* newspaper, BMP advertising campaign
4. *The Observer* newspaper, Viagra
5. Heart Agency calendar

6

7

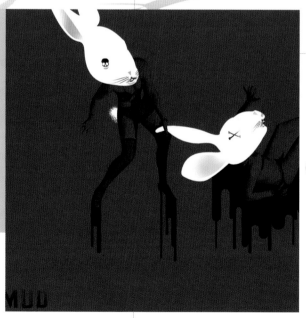

8

6. Kino Design, untitled
7. NB: Studio, Marchant
8. Economist Books, Negotiations

© S. KUBO/2004

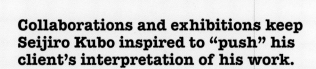

Collaborations and exhibitions keep Seijiro Kubo inspired to "push" his client's interpretation of his work.

Seijiro Kubo made the transition from fully fledged graphic designer to illustrator/image-maker after a friend's chance remark. Upon graduation from the Nippon Designer's School, Kubo worked for a couple of years as a designer for a local graphic design company. By his own admission, he wasn't very good at it, and he decided to quit. "One day, a friend praised some illustrations that I had drawn for work," he states, matter-of-factly, "and that's when I chose to start my career as an illustrator."

Two Solutions
This choice has paid off. Kubo now works for numerous clients and exhibits his own self-initiated work on a regular basis, too. He is confident working in numerous ways, so he approaches each project by creating two

© S. KUBO/2004

1. Flower and Boy, personal project
2. Boy and Friend, personal project

Enjoy 100%, aiwa

We only have now.
So now is the time to play, laugh, enjoy.
Give it 100%.

3

4

Enjoy 100%,

We only have now.
So now is the time to play, laugh, enjoy.
Give it 100%.

versions. "When I am offered a job, I go to meetings with the client to get a clear idea of the work they have in mind," he explains, "then I turn in two drawings. One is the one the client requested, and the other is the one I really want to push. After that, it's up to the client." It is a working method that works, as clients invariably opt for the more extreme versions that Kubo presents. "Basically," he adds, "all my rough drawing is done in an analog style," by which he means working with pencil or pen on paper. "I then do all of the brush-up work on the Macintosh."

Kubo feels most motivated by his work involving the development of characters. He collaborated with Tokyo agency butterfly•stroke for Copet, a Web-based animal adventure playground. This remains a genuinely enjoyable project for him, which he continues to update. Kubo understands the necessity for self-initiated projects such as Copet. The work led directly to a commission for a series of posters for Aiwa, the hi-fi specialists, and brought his work in this medium to new audiences.

The Importance of Freedom
As part of Kubo's drive to push his work into new areas, he constantly exhibits in Tokyo. This gives him the freedom to create new projects involving new ways of working. "For the exhibitions, I tend to draw in a completely new style," he says.

It is clear that Kubo's two areas of work—the professional commissions and the gallery exhibitions—continue to feed each other, but he does recognize a shortfall. "I think I'm a little impatient," he offers, as if waiting for the Mac's digital paint to dry was taking a little too long…

Enjoy 100%.

aiwa

We only have now.
So now is the time to play, laugh, enjoy.
Give it 100%.

Enjoy 100%.

aiwa

We only have now.
So now is the time to play, laugh, enjoy.
Give it 100%.

3. Lion, Aiwa, advertising campaign poster
4. Panda, Aiwa, advertising campaign poster
5. Laforet Grand Bazar 01, advertising campaign poster
6. Laforet Grand Bazar 02, advertising campaign poster
7. Bird, Aiwa, advertising campaign poster
8. Ape, Aiwa, advertising campaign poster

Tutorial 1: Paul Burgess

Breathing new life into old images is an art-form from which Paul Burgess has built a fruitful career. Here he works with lost and found elements to advertise an international fashion retail company.

Paul Burgess has a unique fascination with junk shop, flea market, and secondhand bookstore finds. As indeed he might, with an appetite for creating one-off pieces of artwork that capture a bygone era with a timeless quality, he is the master of the collaged image.

Commissioned by Burro, a fashion label based in Covent Garden in London, Burgess was invited to create an image to run across a double-page spread in US magazine *Sport and Street*. In all, four different artists and designers were invited to create images for the campaign, which ran throughout a summer season. The brief was deceptively simple; Burgess was asked to create an image that conveyed his own interpretation of subjects that included youth culture, the UK, and Pop. Here is how he did that …

1 A found spread from a magazine is pasted onto board to create the base of the image. Burgess then handpaints roughly over areas to obliterate elements, leaving some of the image slightly revealed.

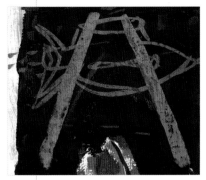

2 A second base area is created using paper that has been painted with gouache. At this point elements are created ready to use, but nothing is added until final design decisions are made.

3 Further base panels are made. This one is from an oddly shaped piece of black card. An important element in Burgess' collages is his lucky finds and how he then plans a usage for these pieces within his work.

4 A cardboard template used to make pom-poms is given a new life as an element in this piece of work. Often Burgess will have images for months before the right project to use them in crops up.

5 The famous Lucky Strike cigarette pack, this one found on the streets of Athens in Greece, is kept in a sketchbook for later use.

6 Scanned, resized, and printed onto acetate, the image forms part of the red circle behind the girl's head. No longer recognizable as a Lucky Strike pack, the image is used purely for its color and shape.

7 As some of the base images are decided upon, they are placed in the final image. Some collage artists like to scan all of their chosen elements into the computer, then resize and reposition each element in Photoshop. For this project, Burgess works by hand.

8 A found drawing, simply titled "Weird Kid," is cut out and detail is added, again by hand. Burgess works with each element lightly tacked in place before putting them together more permanently prior to scanning the final artwork.

9 The background shapes are now formatted and positioned. Burgess understands exactly how the composition may be structured at this stage, having worked out areas of the collage by placing and moving elements around until he is happy with the overall effect.

10 From a magazine found in a flea market in Barcelona, Spain, Burgess scans a drawing of a girl, and makes alterations in Photoshop, changing colors and resizing the image before printing out and trimming to size.

11 Here a section from an old football is removed, partly because of its interesting shape, but also because it has the word "rock" printed on it. It is these kinds of interesting finds that spark creative ideas in the collage artist's mind.

12 Another intriguing element with an interesting history is added to the images being used. An image taken from a long out-of-print children's book about making gifts is scanned, cleaned up, printed out, and utilized.

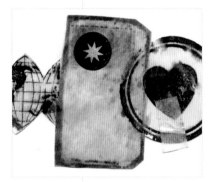

13 Other found elements are incorporated. Motifs of hearts, stars, and globes come together and are "printed" from photocopies using chemical paint thinners to transfer the image: a blurring effect is created using this method.

14 Weird Kid is cut away from any background material, and a touch of redrawing is done to strengthen some of the line work.

15 A similar process occurs with the printout of the girl from Barcelona. Additional handrendered details are added at this stage.

16 Rubber stamps have a unique feel when used in collaged images. Burgess adds a simple graphic to the found bunny before placing the image into the collage.

17 A lettering stencil found in a street market in New York is employed to add some typographic elements by hand. The text is inspired by lyrics from a song by The Libertines.

18 Once elements have slowly built up, the final image starts to take shape and all that remains is for Burgess to either photograph or scan the artwork so that the image file can be sent via e-mail. The image can also be stored as a digital file and Burgess is now free to reuse any of the elements in new work.

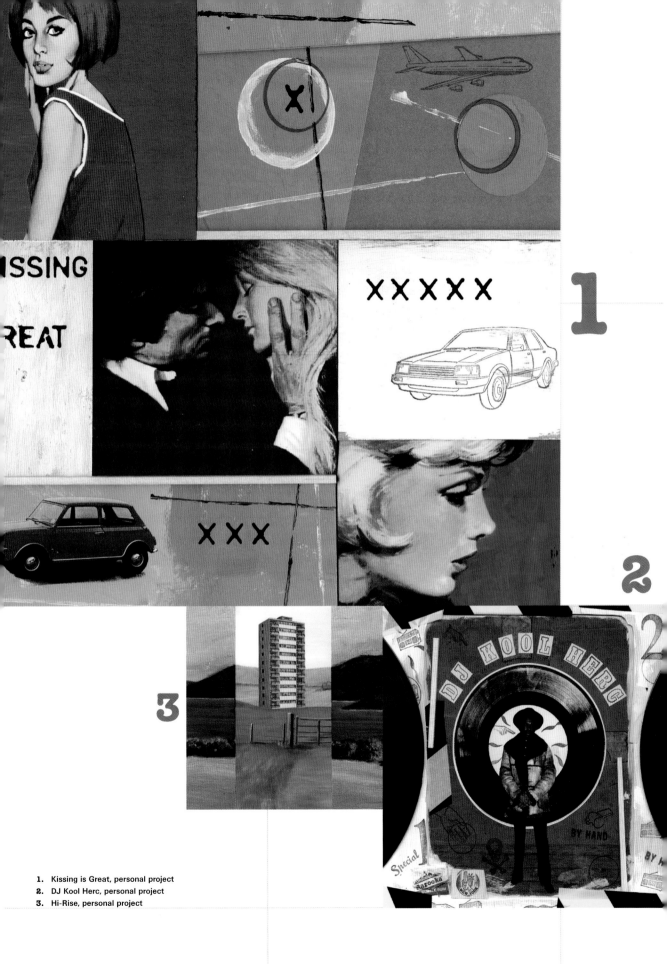

1. Kissing is Great, personal project
2. DJ Kool Herc, personal project
3. Hi-Rise, personal project

Navigator
Cape Tov

GRANGER
BAY

THREE ANCHOR BAY

ROCKLANDS BAY

WESTERN BOULEVARD

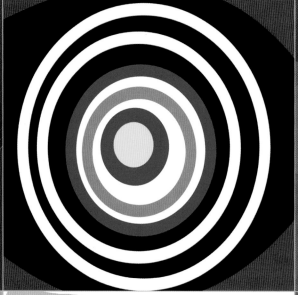

PELUQUERIA

YOU
REAP
WH'T
YOU
Sow

SORTIDA

CA.

PaLM
SPRINGS

AZ.

PhoENIX

TucSon

NM

THIS PUB HAD
BETTER BE
WORTH IT

4

The Power of the Drawn Mark

"Everyone is an artist," claimed Germany's most recognized conceptual artist, Josef Beuys, although it is unclear if his statement extended through to the discipline of drawing.

"Drawing is the honesty of the art. There is no possibility of cheating. It is either good or bad," said Spanish surrealist Salvador Dali. Dali died in 1989, but had he lived into the nineties and witnessed the birth of the digital revolution in design and image-making, he may have found his claim being severely tested. Software applications, emulating the techniques of painting and drawing, became increasingly sophisticated, and for a while it seemed that with the correct kit, the most up-to-the-minute application, and a how-to-do-it book beside the keyboard and drawing tablet, anyone with a modicum of talent could work as a digital artist.

Be an Artist—Be Your own Boss!

Training manuals, proclaiming to teach easy step-by-step lessons in drawing, were not new. In the US during the fifties, with consumerism, mass manufacturing, and mass marketing in abundance, a boom in graphic arts was evident, and advertisements for home-study courses featured in numerous publications. Reproductions of early ads found in *Mostly Happy Clip Art of the Thirties, Forties and Fifties* (Jerry Jankowski, 1992, the Art Direction Book Company, USA) features some prime examples. "stART drawing big money," one proclaims. "Be an artist and be your own boss," another promises, in a drive to attract customers to take up their offer of "commercial art, cartooning, and design—all in ONE practical course. "An ability to draw seemed not to be high on the list of priorities. "Create thousands of your own designs—no lessons, no talent—the first day," was the improbable claim put forward by another advertisement of the time.

1. Jody Barton, Greenpeace, The Last Tree Gone
2. Matthew Green, Sleaze Nation, Nintendo
3. Brian Cairns, Howies, wardrobes
4. Graham Carter, *Televisual* magazine, feature
5. Jason Ford, personal project, Christmas card

6

7

In H. A. Box and T. R. Dipple's book, *How to Draw and Paint Successfully*, also published in the fifties, clear distinctions were made between drawing for pleasure and drawing for profit. "The commercial artist is not selling art but using it to sell something else—a product or service, or even an idea. It is this product, service, or idea that matters most," the book explains. Suggesting that the commercial artist should neither get too precious about the process of drawing nor allow an "artist's ego" to hinder "the principles which govern his work," the book stands as a harsh reality check for those who believed in artistic growth or self-fulfillment through the medium. Despite this, the writers do offer some encouragement to the reader. "A career in commercial art can be interesting, satisfying, and financially rewarding," they state, in a very matter-of-fact manner.

6. Kam Tang, *Dazed & Confused* magazine, PORN?
7. Keiji Ito, VenusFort, advertising campaign
8. Elliott Thoburn, Sleaze Nation, Shoplifting

Art or Illustration?

The debate surrounding commercial artists, later to be viewed as either graphic designers or illustrators, was not a new phenomenon, even in the fifties. Arguments surround 30,000-year-old cave-paintings in Lascaux and Altamira: are they art or illustration? Both sites appear to have been focal points for religious and hunting rites so could be considered to have a functional purpose, highlighting the role of illustration over fine art, perhaps. Even if ancient Chinese picture-writing, Egyptian hieroglyphics, and hand-painted illuminated manuscripts are discounted as the starting point for the printed reproduction of the illustrated image, there is evidence of commercial art as early as the fifteenth century. Printed in 1472, Robertus Valturius produced woodcuts of military and naval equipment in a handbook for military leaders of the Renaissance, and it is known that Leonardo da Vinci owned a copy while he was working as chief engineer to Cesare Borgia. Illustration, unlike painting, did not receive favored recognition. Most Renaissance scholars and humanists regarded it as suitable only for the "vulgar and illiterate," illiteracy being the norm.

Drawn to Drawings

Drawing's link with fine art is inextricable, from Henri Matisse's observation that "drawing is like making an expressive gesture with the advantage of permanence," through to Andy Warhol's opposing description of the activity, as recorded in *The Andy Warhol Diaries*, published in New York in 1989. "I had a picture and I used the tracing machine that projects the image onto the wall and I put the paper where the image is and I trace." Warhol, although later recognized as one of the world's most important modern artists, had originally trained at Carnegie Institute of Technology, where he studied pictorial design. On arriving in New York from Pittsburgh, upon graduation in the summer of 1949, Warhol set to work as a commercial artist and illustrator, with much success.

8

10

11

9

13

14

In *Andy Warhol: Drawings 1942–1987*, Mark Francis and Dieter Koepplin make the assertion, based on the recollections of artist Philip Pearlstein, who graduated with Warhol and moved to New York at the same time, that his success was based on two significant factors. The first was Warhol's "simplicity of style," his work having acquired "its recognizably linear outline and signature economy." The latter was Warhol's "utter willingness to respond to demands from clients." It seems more evidence of the need that commercial artists would have to be willing to sell their own souls to achieve success.

Drawing as a Way of Thinking

Another modern artist, now employing within his work the stark digital graphic techniques most often used in design and illustration disciplines, is Julian Opie. His early drawings and sketches led to the development of his sculptures of household objects, constructed from painted steel. He recorded his own involvement with the discipline of drawing in a catalog accompanying an exhibition of his work at the Institute of Contemporary Art in London in 1985. The publication, a small, pocketbook-sized edition, features an introduction with an insight into Opie's approach. "These drawings are not an attempt to make a pleasing image, or to be finished works in themselves, but rather a way of thinking on paper in a language as immediate as writing," he states. Opie offers a very different take from Warhol on the process of drawing, but his is a valid description of his approach to the process.

12. Shonagh Rae, *Highlife* magazine, Vulture
13. Tom Barwick, Fuck Shit UP Skateboards, Survivalist
14. Tom Gauld, Capsule exhibition, Beer mat

Unlocking the Creative Process

12

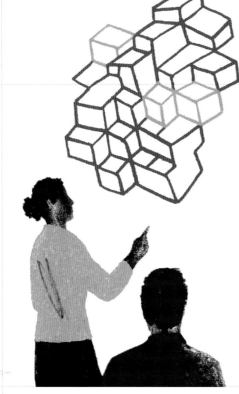

Drawing is a very personal, unique form of practice, whether conducted by the fine artist or the commercial artist. It can come naturally, and it can be improved upon by practice. The impact of real drawing ability, it can be argued, is evidenced in all manner of working methods as employed by today's graphic image-makers. Marshall Arisman, US illustrator and educator for over 40 years, explains in his book *The Education of the Illustrator*, a jointly edited venture with author and art director Steven Heller, that "drawing is an activity that demands practice to realize its full potential." Arisman goes on to state that "a good teacher can help, but drawing is not an end in itself. The process of drawing can unlock the entire creative process for an artist." These are wise words indeed, and a welcome respite from the advertisement claims from a bygone era.

Drawing and the Digital

The relationship that drawing has with the digital remains a sticky subject for some. Arisman explores the issue, stating that he is "fearful that most illustrators' choices about the computer are based on speed, greed, short cuts, and avoiding the practice itself." He suggests that each new drawing contains "memory of our past drawings until we die," adding that it is this memory that separates the activity of drawing from creating an image on the computer. "The tool has no personal memory that is not programmed in," he argues, sidestepping or ignoring the work of those who choose to combine the analog and the digital within their working methods.

It is the work of today's graphic image-makers—those using the mouse to draw, scanning pencil sketches into the computer, combining digital and handmade marks—that is pushing the discipline forward. Whether influenced by the diagrammatic and graphic look of instruction manuals, popular in recent years; simple, pixelated work, reminiscent of early PC screens; or the childlike innocence of "outsider art," it is clear that the drawn image remains as crucial and as inspirational today as it has been for previous generations.

1

1. *Wallpaper** magazine, Netherlands
   navigator map
2. Athlete, *Animals & Vehicles* album cover

The Vector Master who takes one job at a time, perhaps two...

2

For the guy who won a Creative Futures Award for best up-and-coming illustrator in 1998, Kam Tang's first commission was hardly the biggest job on the planet. The brief was for an image that measured 6 x 3cm (2⅜ x 1⅛ in) for a radio listing in the UK's *Radio Times* magazine. In the years since the award, though, Kam Tang has worked for clients in London, Tokyo, New York, Munich, and Amsterdam. Initially, recognized for the finest vector drawing abilities in town, Tang was commissioned by design group Graphic Thought Facility to create illustrations for the annual prospectus of The Royal College of Art (RCA), in London. Tang had studied at the RCA himself and knew how best to represent the hallowed sanctity of the place. He created a vast hand-drawn illustration of the exterior of the building using just a few minimalist vector lines. The real beauty of the piece was in its extremely detailed, full-colored rendering of the ice-cream truck that parked outside the RCA every day. The emphasis of the piece was so wrong yet so right.

Ideas First

Reflecting on his own design approach and philosophy, represented in the early RCA commission, Tang keeps it simple. "Ideas first." This simple approach, coupled with his unmatched vector drawing skills, has impressed a whole range of clients. Tang now counts CD sleeves for Merz, billboard and magazine advertising campaigns for Adidas, and identity work for The Design Museum in London among his favorite commissions.

Work has continued to flood in, and although Tang describes his role simply as "being my own boss and making my own works," it is clear that the flood is not without a certain level of pressure. Juggling deadlines, clients, and commissions from his studio at home in South London, Tang admits, "you can output an incredible amount of work in the final moments of an impending

deadline, but never at the start!" Tang goes on to offer advice to aspiring illustrators, based on his own early experiences. "Never take on more than two jobs at once."

Watching Stanley Kubrick's movies, and old Bruce Lee kung-fu films, listening to Mozart piano sonatas, catching up on comic artworks created by Jack Kirby and George Herriman, and "investigating nature and science," as Tang puts it, are all key aspects of what influences him as an image-maker. New Yorkers Saul Steinberg, Milton Glaser, and Seymour Chwast are all admired by Tang too, but it is perhaps his own left-field take on the world that allowed him to see the beauty in that ice cream truck outside the country's highest seat of art and design learning.

4

MARCH 2005

Wallpaper*

*INTERNATIONAL DESIGN INTERIORS LIFESTYLE

3. Two Culture Clash, *Two Culture Clash* CD sleeve artwork
4. *Wallpaper** magazine, Cape Town navigator map
5. *Wallpaper** magazine, cover illustration

5

Profile: Spencer Wilson

New Resolution Number 1
GIVE UP SMOKING...

1

.... SOMEONE ELSES CIGARETTES.

2

An organized perfectionist, Spencer Wilson's approach and work ethic are, in his own words, "boring."

Spencer Wilson is boring—this is his own description. Reliable or efficient may be a more apt portrayal, although not according to Wilson. "My approach to work has always been quite boring. I always get jobs done on time. I make sure that I never work past 11.00pm, and, if I can, always anticipate what the client may ask for next," he says. "I make a regular point of visiting Zwemmers, Magma, and Waterstones bookstores in London so I can keep abreast of what is happening in design. The last book I bought was *Graphic Design for the 21st Century*. How boring is that?" asks Wilson. This singular vision and professional outlook, combined with a great eye, a sense of humor, and a unique way of working, has assisted Wilson in winning commissions as a busy image-maker.

The Lure of the Personal Project

As one-eleventh of illustration collective Peepshow, Wilson is another image-maker for whom the lure of the personal project and the exhibition is strong. Peepshow have held exhibitions for clients and friends at locations across East London, putting themselves on the map and, at the same time, creating traffic to their group Web site, www.peepshow.org.uk. The members of Peepshow get

3

COME ON

FEEL THE FLOW
PERVERTED EYE FUN

4

5

together once a month to discuss projects and organize exhibitions and publications. These group events help to keep a sense of community in what can be a solitary existence. "The solitude is the toughest thing about working from a studio at home," explains Wilson. "I began working in a large basement living/work space in London, working with two other Peepshow members. The place was dark and rough around the edges, but the positive side was the landlord, a mad ex-photographer, who let us do what we liked," admits Wilson. "I worked on a small desk using a chair I found on the street and an orange iMac, which I loved."

Enjoy the Buzz

Wilson is organized at maintaining contacts. He advises, "see one industry person and get a further three contacts." He keeps in touch with his own clients through regularly e-mailing illustrated images that reflect his current interests and thoughts. A recent piece pictured three advertising creative types around a table responding to the question "How many Art Directors does it take to change a light bulb?" with the witty one-liner, "Does it have to be a light bulb?" It is this type of humor in Wilson's work, along with his neat, quirky, vector-drawn characters, that has led to him working on advertising campaigns for Ski, Buzz Airlines, and Sky Premier. "I enjoy the buzz of being briefed and creating drawings, and I like the lifestyle, working to my own agenda and getting personal projects out there too," explains Wilson, without even a hint of boredom.

6. *Monkey*, personal project, limited-edition book
7. *The Tale of Little Red Riding Hood*, personal project, limited-edition book
8. Science Love, e-mailed promotion

1

1. Diabetes, *The New Yorker*, article
2. I Want You, IKEA USA advertising campaign

2

"No job too large, no job too small, no job too medium-sized." Laurie Rosenwald takes on all comers.

Laurie Rosenwald is a New Yorker through and through, and proud of it. "I'm a native. I was born right here in Manhattan," she exclaims from her huge loft apartment just a couple of paces from the frenetic life of Canal Street. "I grew up in the city. My father was a sculptor, and I was always surrounded by art!" Rosenwald's studio continues the theme. In every direction you see more art: paintings, sculpture, prints, and collections of objects. "I remember wanting to be an artist from an early age, but not a fine artist. Being a fine artist is just trouble. I saw the financial problems my father had as an artist."

All Mushed Together
Rosenwald enrolled on an undergraduate course in graphic design at the Rhode Island School of Design (RISD) because she liked typography, "but it was all Swiss Univers and super-serious and I missed drawing.

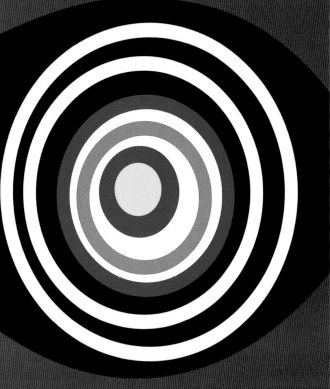

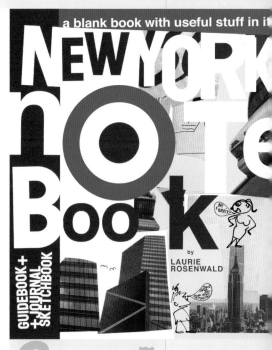

It was so humorless," she recalls. And humor plays a large part in Rosenwald's work, together with her ability to blur edges and resist the lure of the pigeonhole. "I then went into illustration at RISD, but that didn't work. I went back to graphic design but they wouldn't have me, so I went on to painting. They just let me do what I wanted to. Now what I do is painting, typography, and illustration all mushed together."

Digital Love–Hate

Nowadays, Rosenwald divides her time between her loft in Manhattan and Sweden, where she shares studio space with a group of artists and designers, following an artist-in-residence program she attended a few years ago. Despite technology making life and travel easier—she works on an Apple PowerBook that goes everywhere with her—she has a love–hate relationship with computers. "The computer brings people together in one way and alienates them in another. I can create work in Sweden for a client in Philadelphia but never meet them, or hear their voice; it is all done by e-mail. I still find that strange."

New York—Soup to Nuts

Every project of Rosenwald's, although finalized and transmitted digitally, starts with drawing. She draws by hand using a dip pen and ink, often making up to 100 drawings. She likes to progress straight to the finished product, so rarely creates visuals or roughs for clients. "I don't do sketches; I just do it. It can be a pain though: I sometimes feel I'm reinventing the wheel every time I start a commission." Her approach has attracted a range of clients that includes *The New Yorker*, Ikea, and Coca-Cola, but it is her own book, *New York Notebook*, which she wrote and designed, that has fired her imagination. "People have always come to stay," she states. "I'm always giving folk advice about what to see and do. It made sense to put it in a book. New York—soup to nuts!"

5

Photo Graphic Image-Making

With edges starting to blur and the boundaries between skills far less distinct, the graphic image-maker, in incorporating digital photographic images in his/her work, stands across the divide between two disciplines.

Contemporary image-makers know no boundaries. They employ a range of techniques, whenever appropriate, without fear of crossing borders or demarcations between disciplines. As confident with a mouse as a pencil, as savvy with a drawing tablet as a digital camera, they fearlessly adopt and adapt processes and methods of working with little regard for the historical baggage that accompanies some aspects of art, design, and photography. This freedom stems from being at the forefront of a discipline that does not follow a single medium of expression, thus allowing the image-maker opportunities for crossover and the merging of processes. Following migration from the analog to the digital, many image-makers turned their attention to formats that would capture real life and that could be returned to the studio ready and available for editing and modifying. The answer lay with the digital camera.

Believe in Photographs

At the dawn of traditional photography, the medium struggled to gain recognition as an independent art form; it was viewed to be in direct opposition to painting. Historically, reactions have been less than positive. Picasso proclaimed, "I have discovered photography. Now I can kill myself. I have nothing else to learn."

Years later, British photographer David Bailey hit back, "It takes a lot of imagination to be a good photographer. You need less imagination to be a painter, because you can invent things. But in photography everything is so ordinary; it takes a lot of looking before you learn to see the ordinary." Ansel Adams, US photographer and environmentalist, recorded his views, "Not everybody trusts paintings, but people believe photographs," he stated.

1. Neasden Control Centre, Agent Deck/Rome Snowboards, skate deck design
2. Shonagh Rae, personal project, Australia
3. Insect, personal project, POW Poster—01
4. Insect, personal project, POW Poster—02
5. Insect, personal project, POW Poster—03

2

3

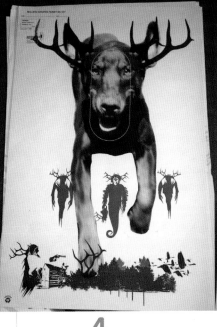

4

5

In commercial design, advertising, and publishing, the photographer, it would appear, has always been held in greater regard than the illustrator, commanding higher fees, demanding expenses, and hiring and firing assistants. The mystique surrounding the professional photographer has been utilized to great effect. Mainly due to the perceived complexities of camera and darkroom equipment, this technology has served to reinforce preconceptions. As the PC and associated desktop publishing boom of the late eighties and nineties opened the medium to the home user, so too did the introduction of the digital camera. Digital advances, quite simply, changed the landscape of photography.

From Spy Satellites to Video Freeze-Frame

The digital camera has its origins in spy satellites, with government backing in digital technology, but the private sector also made major contributions. Texas Instruments were the first to patent a filmless electronic camera, in 1972, and nine years later, Sony released the Sony Mavica electronic still camera. The first commercial electronic camera, it recorded images onto a mini disc that had to be put into a video reader connected to a TV monitor or color printer. Despite kickstarting a revolution, the Sony Mavica can't truly be considered a digital camera; it was a video camera that took video freeze-frames.

Kodak, working to advance digital technology since the mid-seventies, had invented several solid-state image sensors that would convert light to digital pictures, but it wasn't until 1986 that Kodak scientists announced the world's first megapixel sensor. Capable of recording 1.4 million pixels, the sensor could produce a 7 x 5in digital, photo-quality print. In 1987, Kodak released seven new products for recording, storing, manipulating, transmitting, and printing electronic still video images. In 1990 they introduced the Photo CD system and with that, developed the first global standard for defining color in the digital environment. In 1991, Kodak launched the first truly digital camera system (DCS), aimed at professional photojournalists, in the shape of the Nikon F3 camera. This was fully equipped with a 1.3-megapixel sensor.

8

9

10

6. Andy Martin, Heart Care, *The Observer* newspaper, article
7. David Foldvari, Weiden Kennedy, private commission, untitled
8. Mutador, Belio, Energias Renovadas exhibition image
9. ilovedust, *Computer Arts* magazine, NYC Block
10. Tim Marrs, *The Guardian* newspaper, Miami

11
12
13

14

15

16

The "Serial Killer"

Consumers had to wait another four years for a camera that would work with a home computer. Apple, in another industry coup, launched the Apple QuickTake 100 camera in February 1994 at the MacWorld Expo in Tokyo, 10 years after the groundbreaking Macintosh had arrived. Shaped like a pair of binoculars and finished stylishly in matte gray, the QuickTake 100 introduced a new file format, QuickTake, that used QuickTime to decompress images. Dubbed the "serial killer" due to the camera's "plug and play" connectivity via a simple cable rather than the complicated SCSI connections found in all other peripheries of the time, the camera worked on both Mac and PC platforms. A review of the Apple QuickTake 100 in *Digital Imaging Plus* magazine, one month after Apple's launch of the camera, reads like the first reviews of the iMac and iPod years later, describing the camera as a "simple but well designed 'sexy' product that is fun and easy to use." The reviewer saw the future in the QuickTake 100. "If it catches on, it will be the forerunner of a line of products which could change the way that families take, manage, and print their social pictures," they predicted.

Despite Apple standing on the brink of a digital photography revolution, the QuickTake 100 would prove, as *Digital Imaging Plus* magazine had predicted, to be just the "forerunner" of advances in new digital camera technology. A year into Apple's lead in this key aspect of the digital domain, Kodak launched the DC40. This was followed by Casio's premier of their QV-11, the first digital camera with an LCD monitor, later the same year. Sony entered the market in 1996, with the Cyber-shot digital still camera. However, it was Kodak, aided by a huge marketing campaign, that put digital photography in the public consciousness. In collaboration with Microsoft and Kinkos, Kodak created digital image-making software kiosks and workstations, enabling customers to create photo CD discs, enhance and manipulate photographs, and add digital images to documents. Soon after, Hewlett-Packard launched the first color printers designed to complement digital camera images. Where the Polaroid camera, invented by American physicist Edwin Land and first launched in 1948, had offered the public instant images, the digital camera went many steps further.

Radical Shifts

The digital camera is perhaps so remarkable because it has been such a radical shift from its predecessor. Dependent on chemical and mechanical processes, the conventional camera uses a series of lenses that focus light onto a piece of film to create an image. The digital camera, also through the use of lenses, focuses light onto an image sensor that records electronically; a computer then translates this information into digital data. With camera prices falling, specifications improving, and digital photographic images in a format easily imported into editing software, it has been no surprise that photography and graphic image-making have begun to merge so seamlessly in recent years.

As a reference tool, the digital camera has proven invaluable: easy-to-use, small, portable, and relatively inexpensive to purchase. For the image-maker who draws from visual reference materials, bringing instant images into the computer as a starting point is a straightforward process. Taking one's own images, rather than relying on printed reference material in books, means that there is no shadow of copyright infringement. Taking away the reliance on images from stock reference libraries

or trawling the Web gives back much of the creativity to the image-maker. Setting up, taking images, and importing them into the relevant software application to use as reference material has become second nature to many contemporary creative image-makers.

Blurring Edges

For those who choose to work more directly with the photographic image, incorporating it into their work or making it the main aspect of their creative process, rather than using it simply as a source of reference material, the digital camera has helped create entirely new working methods and results. The introduction of screen printing into fine art, in the early sixties, could be viewed as a forerunner to this approach. Artists in the US, among them Robert Rauschenberg, used the process of screen printing to bring a raw realism to picture-making through the use of the photographic in combination with paint and collage. Here was a technique that allowed the direct reproduction of a photographic image onto the surface of a painting or collage. The digital camera, combined with the computer and associated software applications, has given the image-maker the same powers within the digital domain.

As edges blur and the distinctions between boundaries become less well defined, questions are being asked about the role of the photographer and the illustrator. Where these areas of crossover merge, bleeding from one to another, is where today's image-makers stand.

18

19

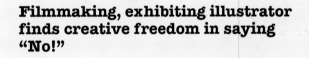

1

2

1. Host, *Libération* magazine, feature
2. Heart of Chairs, *The Observer* newspaper, article

Filmmaking, exhibiting illustrator finds creative freedom in saying "No!"

Joe Magee has lived in many cities in the UK. Having studied in his hometown of Liverpool before moving on to the London College of Printing and then, at MA level, Manchester Metropolitan University, Magee has finally made Bristol his home. His name is now inseparably linked, across the city, with an exhibition he held at Watershed Arts Centre, Bristol's cultural melting pot. People often say "ah yes, the rabbits," as they nod in recognition if you mention Magee's name. The rabbits were part of an animated piece about memetics and mind viruses which included endlessly replicating white rabbits on a red background. These have, according to Magee, "found their way into many people's psyches. So the idea seems to have worked."

Independent Thinking

Magee's images garner responses from his audience. He provokes reactions through his work, and finds he is commissioned because his work has a point of view. He cites his most memorable job as the Penguin cover for Anthony Burgess' novel *A Clockwork Orange*. His heroes include Peter Saville, Andy Warhol, Vincent Van Gogh, David Lynch, and William Heath Robinson, so it is clear that he has a high regard for other independent thinkers and creators.

Having utilized digital media for many years, Magee has developed a creative visual within his images that imbues them with an individuality, a unique look and feel.

Magee puts this down to retaining creative freedom. "I've never been motivated by making lots of money, and I think this has really helped facilitate creative development. I've always felt compelled to remain independent and tried to feel comfortable about what jobs I'll accept. The reality of saying 'no' to big bucks for an artistically or ethically challenged job is harsh, but always feels good in the end," he explains.

Independent Projects
Magee works at a prolific rate. He has to, with two illustrations for national newspapers to create every week of the year, before he takes anything else on. Other Illustration commissions continue to arrive on a regular basis. "I've always had a steady stream of work from the US, having worked for *The New York Times*, *The Boston Globe*, and the *Los Angeles Times*. I've also worked regularly for *Libération* in France for many years."

It is extra-curricular projects that keep Magee motivated. Recently completed are three award-winning films about addictive behavior set on a deprived housing estate. "I'm becoming more and more interested in making films. I've found it difficult to stop making films. I've made about 10 in the last five years and am getting more commissioned," explains Magee. On top of the illustration and filmmaking, Magee exhibits. "I like the freedom in taking on independent, noncommercial projects, like generating a series of large digital prints for an exhibition at an interesting gallery," he says.

This is one independent, filmmaking, gallery-exhibiting illustrator who will continue to make the most of his creative freedom.

4

5

93

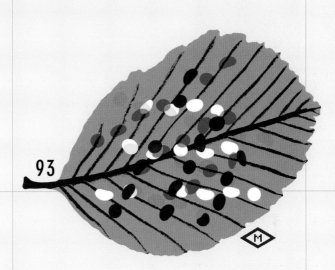

6

3. Clique, *The Observer* newspaper, article
4. Eden500, personal project, interactive digital artwork
5. Leaf Virus, *The Guardian* newspaper, article
6. Blackbird, personal project, digital artwork

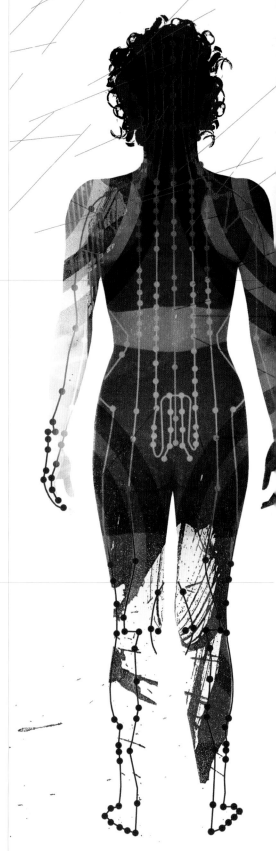

1

Mellow jazz, sixties' graphics, and the spirit of collaboration push the right buttons for McFaul, a man who time forgot.

"I've always been interested in and influenced by graphic image-makers; Saul Bass, Paul Rand, Woody Pirtle, and Kurt Schwitters. That whole generation of designers and artists who really kicked off in the sixties," explains McFaul from his newly converted loft/studio. Sitting in a chair that can best be described as a "we've been expecting you Mr. Bond" affair, with the mellow jazz sounds of Craig Armstrong playing in the background, McFaul could easily be mistaken for the man who time forgot. Until you see his work, that is.

Graphical Thinking

"I think quite graphically. I start with doodles that represent my thinking and move onto a list of ingredients," states McFaul, recounting a process that might equally describe the work of a jazz musician. "I collaborate with designers, rather than working for them," he muses. "I'm interested in the process over the esthetic," However, the esthetic remains crucial within his work—a beautiful synergy of the drawn and the photographic merged with pattern, with color, and with skill and dexterity that belies McFaul's origins in the print studio. "My work has been arrived at through the time I spent printmaking," he explains. "I enjoyed the experimentation and the things that went wrong; in fact, if it went wrong, it was so right."

1. I'm Thinking of Tron, *The Economist* magazine, feature
2. Winter, *Digital Creative Arts* magazine, cover image

From Analog to Digital

The migration from analog to digital worlds was a relatively painless operation brought about by necessity. "I began getting too much work. I just thought, I can do color separations in minutes and hours on screen, rather than days in the print studio," McFaul admits. Having worked on a PC before moving to Apple, he now works across three machines in his studio, and uses a laptop when on the road.

Never without his camera, McFaul travels most places with it, his laptop, and an external drive in a bag. "I shoot stuff all of the time, every day," he explains. "I use figures in my work; they're generally friends, family—people I know mostly, although I do have to shoot some people without their knowledge," McFaul states, describing his use of the figure as if it were simply part of his list of chosen ingredients. A recent client, Publix, a supermarket chain based in Florida, commissioned McFaul to create a range of packaging for their sodas, and some tight restrictions forced a new approach. For the first time, working with a professional model, he was able to seek out someone of the exact profile described in the client brief.

Technology Enabled

It is where the edges between disciplines meet and blur that now interests McFaul. "I see more and more photographers digitally manipulating their images, and more and more illustrators using digital photography," he explains. "As image-makers, we can do anything that we want; the technology now allows it." McFaul celebrates the freedom open to today's graphic image-maker. "At art school, I could draw, so tutors actively pushed me toward illustration, but what I needed was the freedom to explore graphic design, fine art, illustration, and photography. And that's all I do now. The point is in doing something new every day." And right on cue, like the title of a hit by a sixties' jazz ensemble, he adds "It's what life is all about!"

3. Love, *Men's Health* magazine, Germany, feature
4. Love, *Men's Health* magazine, Germany, feature
5. *Mind Wide Open*, book jacket

1

2

Profile:
Josh Gosfield

It is a surreal journey that has led Josh Gosfield to the Mighty House of Pictures. "It's a pleasure to serve you."

It wasn't always this way for Josh Gosfield. As an untrained graphic designer—unless a year spent studying Agricultural Engineering at Cornell University in Ithaca, upstate New York counts—he arrived in New York City to work as a magazine art director. "I've always taught myself everything," Gosfield admits. "The bottom of the learning curve is where I like to be," he adds with a smile.

In 1994, after an eight-year stint as Art Director on *New York* magazine, Gosfield left commercial design to work as an image-maker. He has never regretted the move. "I was possessed of the naive misconception that the work would be done in some highly creative hothouse environment," Gosfield states. "I enjoyed the social aspect, the late-night deadline pressure, but I found the experience corporate, hierarchical, and often boring."

Life is anything but boring now. In a strangely corporate offices-to-rent building, a few blocks from the Holland Tunnel entrance in Manhattan, is Gosfield's studio—a manic and chaotic space where he busily employs a vast range of media. Surrounded by plaster-cast models, boxes of toys, theater props, and thrift-store cast-offs, along with vast numbers of aging magazines, books, and posters, Gosfield creates work with a passionate energy.

1. Saint of the Month: Castor/Pollux, personal project
2. Cat Girls, personal project

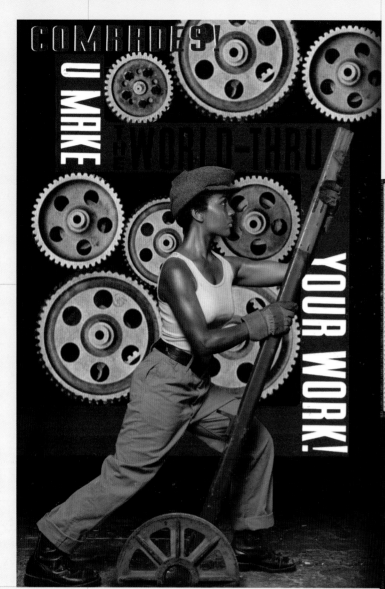

3

4

5

From Warsaw to Rwanda
From Wall Street to Baghdad

JOSHGOSFIELD.COM

ST. LIZETTE REMEMBERS
All Those Who Fall to
Bullets, Bayonets and Bombs

From Fine Art to Commercial Art

Working across disciplines, stepping from fine art into commercial art and back again, whether making installations for the windows of Barney's, (New York City's coolest fashion department store, in Chelsea), or creating artworks for MTV, Nike, Levi's, or Sony, Gosfield happily breaks the mold. "I love everything. I love learning the new thing. I love combining various art forms," he exclaims. "Maybe it's self-sabotage, but as soon as I start getting comfortable with a craft, I get bored and want to move on." Gosfield admits to a demanding working process. "The thrill factor, for me, is higher when I really don't know what I'm doing."

A Brutal Ecstasy

Not knowing what he's doing includes shooting his subjects for inclusion in an image on a Nikon DX1 camera. "I'm mostly digital now. The digital world is changing so fast that it's a blast to be hooked up to all of that," he states, in a manner that belies his knowledge of the subject. With a Web site that welcomes the visitor to The Mighty House of Pictures, gallantly offering "It's a pleasure to serve you" as the corporate mantra, Gosfield is aware of his influences. The site, itself credits "all the great artists and hacks, Mexican sign painters, prison tattoo artists, and pornographers" who have inspired him. "Maybe it's a kind of brutal ecstasy I'm thrown into by great art, or moments in life," he suggests. "It could as easily be a guy loping down the street with a cocky gait and a hat cocked at an insane angle on his head as it can a painting."

Recent projects show Gosfield diversifying once again; he has written, produced, directed, edited, and scored a 20-minute, live-action film that is doing the rounds of the independent film festivals. He is still in search of the next dream project. "I have too many to list—theater sets, feature-length film, giant photos on lightboxes, huge altars in Times Square …" All very far removed from magazine art direction or agricultural engineering.

Tutorial 2: McFaul

Increasingly, McFaul finds himself commissioned because of the blend of processes and techniques he employs.

Virgin Atlantic commissioned McFaul to work on a project that involved creating images to be used as stickers for VIP baggage, as a limited-edition, signed and numbered poster/print, and for use on a select range of T-shirts. With the design company involved in the project based in Miami, and McFaul based in the UK, communication and liaison was done via e-mail and the Web. McFaul describes the project as a "dream job." The client, a big fan of his approach, kept expanding the commission into new media as they became increasingly excited with his work.

McFaul uses a combination of techniques that derive from his initial use of the camera; he often shoots his own models and materials for a project. His working process then involves taking these digital images back to the studio for manipulating in Photoshop and Illustrator. The results speak for themselves.

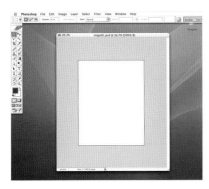

1 The blank canvas, or in this case the white of the screen, is always a daunting start for the image-maker. This is where it all begins.

2 In Photoshop, the entire screen is filled with a color picked from the Virgin palette of chosen hues. The process of selecting and starting with a base color kicks the image off.

3 The client, Virgin Atlantic, have provided some visual material. This image of the interior of an aircraft is too small to be of any real use in the final image, but acts as a useful reference point.

4 While the supplied photograph can't be used within the artwork—the file resolution is too low—the image can be vector traced in Illustrator.

5 Further vector tracing starts to identify seats and windows within the image. Subtle use of line ensures that these background shapes give a sense of the location, but not in any great detail at this stage.

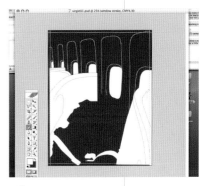

6 Further work starts to visually describe elements of the interior. This aspect of the process can be time-consuming, but attention to detail is vital.

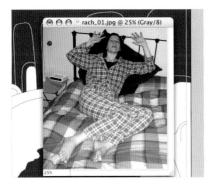

7 A photographic image, one of McFaul's own, is imported into the document. McFaul shoots real people as visual reference. This image is to be a startlet waking from a restful slumber on board a Virgin flight from London to Los Angeles.

8 The photographic reference is traced using vector lines as shown previously. Once an image is in the computer, it can become integral to the working process.

9 With superfluous details removed, the photographic image is imported into the original artwork file. The girl now appears to be waking in the Virgin interior.

10 The nature of the brief demands that the final image is maximalist and decadent in look and feel. Here McFaul creates a linear gradient in white. He treats gradients, blurs, and layer blending with sensitivity: too much and the image can look overworked.

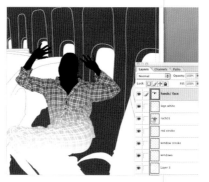

11 The composition is adjusted. Flipping the figure fits the piece better. It is always a good idea to spend time making images from various sources look convincing.

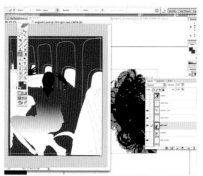

12 At this point McFaul adds elements of vector art from what he calls his armory—a folder on his computer. Having images to hand can save valuable time that would otherwise have to be spent redrawing.

13 A number of Illustrator vector files are combined to create the hair on the model, contributing to the sense of the "starlet."

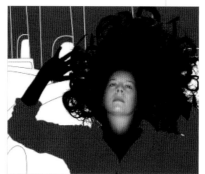

14 A face is imported into the image to give some kind of reality to the figure. This is done quite roughly at this stage—improvements will be made later.

15 Further manipulation takes place, improving the image through blending modes and working with channels. This is the best route in getting under the skin of an application.

16 The image has to have a really strong graphic quality, so it makes sense to adjust the look of the pyjamas. By removing the check from the pyjamas and replacing it with vertical stripes, the shape of the body will be better defined.

17 Removing the horizontal lines is time-consuming, but an hour spent working in Photoshop will resolve the pyjamas visually. They are a vital aspect of the image and so demand this level of attention.

18 The effect of the pinstripes is to flatter the woman's figure and to suggest cosiness—exactly the values that Virgin are looking to communicate.

19 Stars and ribbons are added from the "armory" to give a more magical feel to the image. Importing vector images from Illustrator into Photoshop is a simple procedure and makes best use of the differences in the applications.

20 An additional ingredient is brought into the image; this time snow adds to the overall effect, imported as Illustrator files once again.

21 The composition is checked and rechecked, and the figure moved slightly to the right. These subtle shifts can make all the difference.

22 Some further work on the face, sensitively playing with the blending modes and channels on several layers, creates a look more in keeping with the feel of the image.

23 One aspect of the brief detailed the importance of including the flight number, 24, and the Virgin logo on the pyjamas. These are considered during the design stages, but only added toward the end of the process.

24 The logo is imported, with some skewing and retouching undertaken to create an element that sits well visually within the context of the image. This is a time-consuming process; blending photographic reference with digital drawing can take time.

1. Love, *Men's Health* magazine, Germany, feature

Working Process

Commerical Image-Making

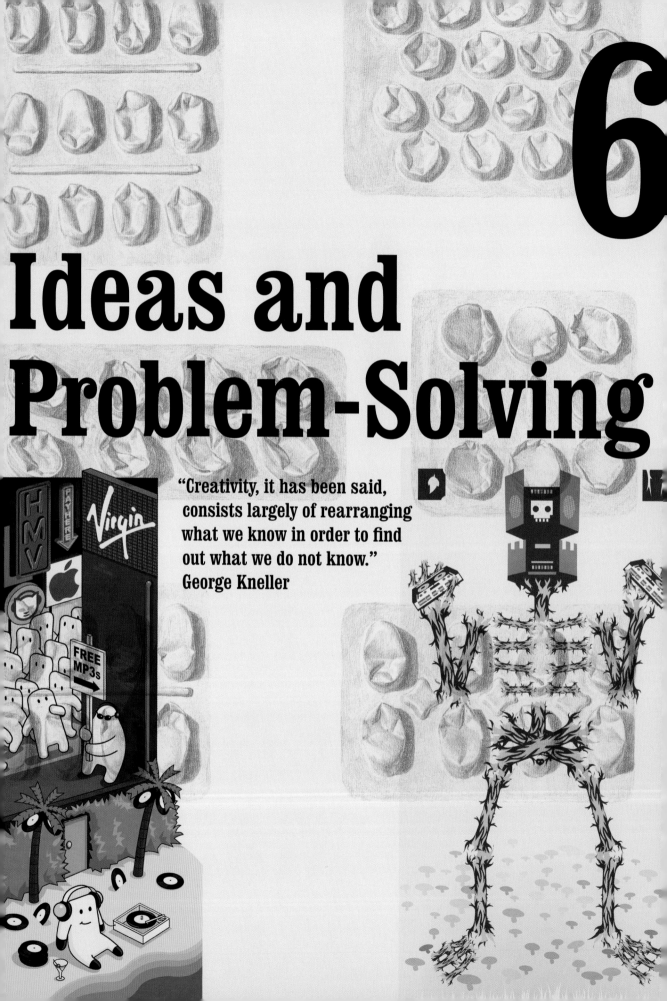

Ideas and Problem-Solving

6

"Creativity, it has been said, consists largely of rearranging what we know in order to find out what we do not know."
George Kneller

Creative-thinking concepts

What is creative thinking? What is an idea and how do we distinguish a good idea from a bad one? From where do we draw our inspiration? How can we ensure that we avoid hitting the visual equivalent of writer's block when faced with the whiteness of the paper or the blankness of the screen when we embark on a new project?

"Imagination is more important than knowledge." These words were uttered, not by an artist or designer as one might expect, but by a physicist, albeit the world's greatest physicist—Albert Einstein. Named Person of the Century by *Time* magazine in 1999, "Einstein" has become synonymous with "genius," so his words should not be ignored.

Einstein's views are supported by another great thinker; Edward De Bono, noted psychologist and physician. The phrase "thinking outside the box" has become part and parcel of De Bono's theories on creative thinking and the value of ideas. He has explored these theories across numerous books, at last count over 75; advised corporations such as IBM, Shell, Eriksson, and Coca-Cola; and taught at rural schools in South Africa and villages in Cambodia.

1

1. Paul Blow, *Design Week*, "Choice," front cover.
2. Nathan Daniels, 1576 Agency, T-shirt design.

"Imagination is more important than knowledge." These words were uttered, not by an artist or designer as one might expect, but by a physicist, albeit the world's greatest physicist—Albert Einstein.

2

3

"Sometimes I just stare at the white page," explains illustrator Paul Blow, "and literally have to force an idea to come." However, over a decade of illustrating experience has taught him not to panic.

An art form

It is all well and good getting to grips with concepts of creative thinking, but illustration, and the creation of images in response to a brief may be considered less a science and more an art form. And art forms don't always go according to plan. "Sometimes I just stare at the white page," explains illustrator Paul Blow, "and literally have to force an idea to come." However, over a decade of experience as an illustrator has taught him not to panic. "Once the initial blockage is cleared, the ideas come reasonably rapidly. With the hard work over, then comes the fun of working out the compositions and design." Blow's working process begins with a mix of creative thinking and brainstorming, exploring thoughts and concepts based on how he wishes to interpret the copy he is illustrating. With a clutch of illustration awards to his credit, his ideas—and his ability to visualize them in creative and stylish ways—have snared an array of clients across the globe, from the *Financial Times* and the BBC to *Time* magazine, *LA* magazine, and the *Harvard Business Review*. Blow's final solutions are well considered and well executed, but the lead-up to the end result may be anything but carefully planned. "I'm always keen to let accidents happen," he admits, "particularly when creating my own personal work for exhibitions. I really let my imagination run wild."

4

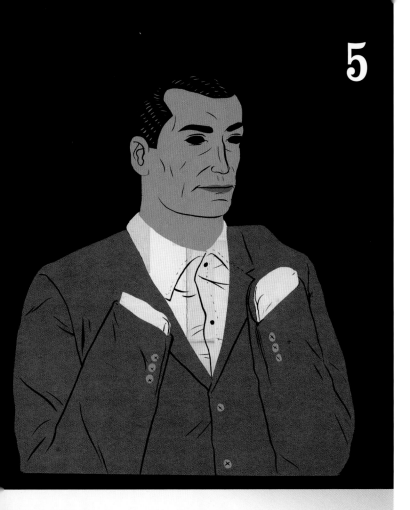

5

Imagination and ideas

"I've climbed Mount Everest without oxygen," begins Edvard Scott from his studio in Stockholm, Sweden, "I've seen *Titanic* on the bottom of the ocean, I've fought my way through the blistering cold of Siberia on a bike, I've journeyed the desert of the Sahara on a camel, and I've painted smiley faces on the statues at Easter Island." For a moment it seems that Scott appears to have a loose grip on reality, until he adds his final one-liner. "I'm 21 years old and it is all about imagination." Having the ability to be imaginative, creative, and push ideas forward isn't easily quantifiable.

The word idea comes from a Greek term meaning "I saw," which picks up on the concept that an idea is an image formed in the mind. Creativity is best described as a mental process involving the generation of new ideas and concepts, and this process, scientists believe, can be broken down into two pathways: convergent and divergent. It is believed that scientists and engineers typically display convergent thinking when resolving a problem. This is generally recognized as the deductive generation of the best single answer to a problem. However, it is believed that artists and performers display a tendency for divergent thinking; the creative generation of multiple answers to a problem.

6

3.   George Myers, *Manners*, personal project.
4.   Andy Rementer, *Clark Magazine*, front cover.
5.   Paul Blow, untitled, personal project.
6.   Edvard Scott, Royal Festival Hall, Rhythm, ad.

Brainstorming tips and tricks

Divergent thinking can be best utilized as a basis for creative brainstorming, first popularized as a catalyst for creativity in the late 1930s. Alex Faickney Osborn, an advertising executive and one of the founders of global advertising agency BBDO, encouraged brainstorming for this purpose. While it hasn't been scientifically proven, it has certainly caught on as a term to describe the free-form generation of ideas. There are four basic rules for brainstorming:

1. focus on quantity;
2. don't criticize;
3. welcome unusual ideas; and
4. combine and improve ideas.

The first aims to enhance divergent thinking. The second, particularly useful for group brainstorming sessions, emphasizes positive feedback, thus fostering an environment for greater, risk-free creativity. The third looks to aid the out-of-the-box thinking that may lead to new and unconventional problem solving. The fourth is based on the belief that better solutions can emerge from a combination of ideas rather than the generation of ideas in isolation.

7

8

7. David Sparshott, MAKE, "MAKE Architect's Annual 2006," editorial.

8. Daniel Mitchell, *The Travelling Cowboy*, personal project.

9. Joe McLaren, *Fifteen Minutes In the Garden Of Eden*, personal project.

10. Yuko Kondo, Merrydown, *Up Side Down*, poster.

11. Paul Blow, Eastwing illustration agency, *Ghost Writer*, ad.

12. Nathan Daniels, *Virus*, personal project.

FIFTEEN MINUTES IN THE GARDEN OF EDEN
A NEW PLAY BY GUY WOODHOUSE
EVESHAM ARTS CENTRE
SUN 14 JAN 2007
8.30pm £3.50

9

Don't be right—be wrong

Paul Arden, formerly Executive Creative Director for Saatchi & Saatchi, and responsible for numerous award-winning campaigns for British Airways, Toyota, and the *Independent*, explores simple tips for creative thinking in his book *It's Not How Good You Are, It's How Good You Want To Be*. Arden argues that you don't have to be creative to be creative, and promotes the sense that most creative problem solving is a logical process. Arden's approach to creative thinking begins with the advice, "Start being wrong and suddenly anything is possible," and continues, "You're in the unknown. There's no way of knowing what can happen, but there's more chance of it being amazing than if you try to be right. Of course, being wrong is a risk." Stepping into the unknown, challenging preconceptions, and taking a left-field approach are all part of Arden's powerful creative-thinking techniques.

Arden argues that you don't have to be creative to be creative. His approach to creative thinking begins with the advice, "Start being wrong and suddenly anything is possible."

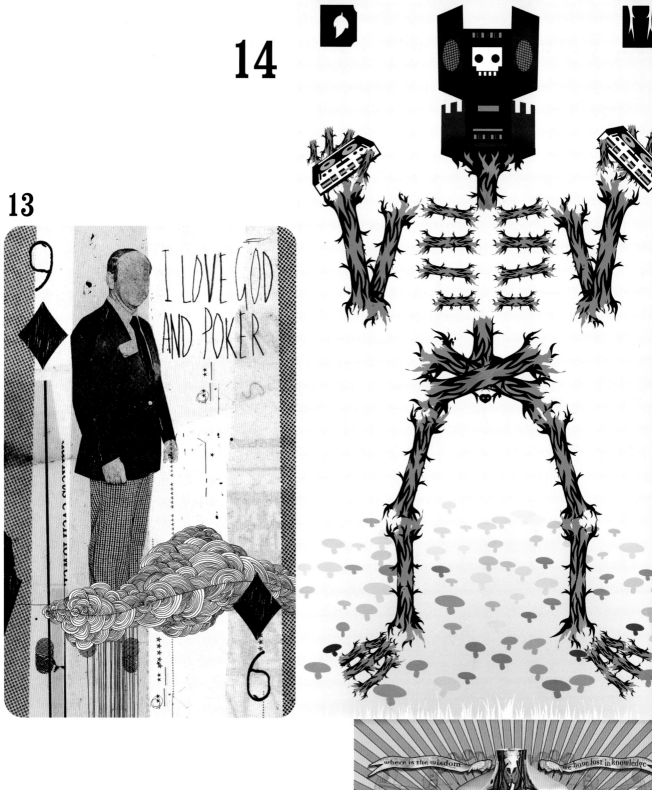

13

14

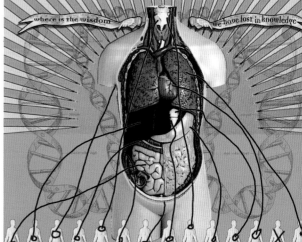

15

Doing the opposite

But what happens when it is all going wrong and the deadline is fast approaching? "We all get mental blocks," Arden writes. "The way to get unblocked is to lose our inhibitions and stop worrying about being right." Arden offers a few solutions to free the flow of ideas. "If you are in a deadlock, here are a couple of tricks you might try. 1. Do the opposite of what the solution requires; and 2. Look out the window and whatever catches your eye, a bird, a television aerial, an old man on crutches, make that the solution."

People sometimes make the move from advertising into illustration, keen to explore new methods of creativity, away from the frustrations of client demands, the interruptions and expectations of account handlers, and the feeling that they play only a small role within a much larger team. Kerry Roper is one such creative who made the move. Having studied design and advertising, he worked as an advertising art director before embarking on a career as an illustrator. This background has had an undeniable influence on the development of his ideas. "Working in an ad agency taught me to ensure that ideas communicate quickly and effectively." Roper's clients now include advertising agencies—he has created illustrations for Snickers and Nike campaigns. His solution to finding creative solutions is, "Think, think, think, and then just go for it. I usually just follow my instincts when it comes to finding a solution," he admits.

Archives and inspirations

For most illustrators, however, it is not simply about sitting and thinking with a pen and paper. Many have extensive libraries of influences and inspirations, built up over a period of time. This could be images that kick-start a chain of thought; it could be a strange mix of overprinted colors on a used ticket stub; it could just as easily be a juxtaposition of typographic elements and images on a gig poster or club flyer that influences a way of working. The trigger for an idea can often occur through a mix of inspirations and perspiration.

16

Ayşegül Özmen, born and based in Istanbul, Turkey, understands the importance of her archives of "inspirations." "I like to browse through my personal archive in order to inspire and influence my designs or illustrations," she reflects. Özmen trained in Fine Art in Istanbul before enrolling in a course in Computer Graphics Design in the US, returning to her home city to study graphic design further before completing a PhD. "I approach the client's brief, find out its needs, and from that moment on I start to think about the illustration. Key words are a great help as well as inspiration sources. I like to tell a story with visual details. For me it is important for the viewer to spend some time looking at the image and determining and understanding the story."

13. Kerry Roper, 9 Sushi Project, *Defaced Playing Card*, ad.
14. George Myers, HiFi Club, Leeds, *Deadwood: Creature*, ad.
15. Ayşegül Özmen, *New Perspectives*, "Organ Cloning," editorial.
16. Alice Stevenson, *Woods*, personal project.
17. Fairoz Noor, Tiger Beer, King of the Animal Kingdom, ad.

17

Tiger

Human nature

Peter James Field entered image-making on completing a formal design education. It was his previous studies, however, that helped shape his approach. Field studied anthropology and worked as a teacher before returning to his own education and embarking on his subsequent career as an illustrator. "Things that inspire me vary all of the time, from plastic painkiller packets to the 1960s brutalism of car-park architecture, to reality TV, via pretty much anything else. In my work," he continues, "I'm not interested so much in decorating things or looking for hidden order or obvious beauty. Show me a gorgeous landscape, and I'll look for the place where people dump litter and draw that. It's more interesting. It tells us more about human nature." This last comment is a clear indication that Field's background in anthropology has helped shape his inspirations.

"Things that inspire me vary all of the time, from plastic painkiller packets to the 1960s brutalism of car-park architecture, to reality TV, via pretty much anything else."

19

The route to individuality

Whatever route an illustrator takes to inspiration and creative thinking, it is clear that those who succeed in the discipline have the ability to combine strong ideas with a unique visual approach—they have their own personal visual language. Without both criteria equally matched, it is unlikely an illustrator will succeed. As Herman Melville, poet and novelist responsible for the literary classic *Moby Dick*, said, "It's better to fail in originality, than succeed in imitation."

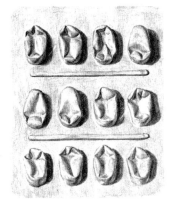

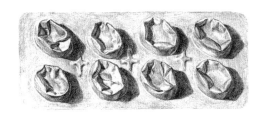

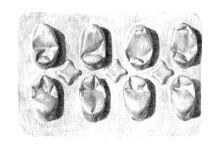

18. Nathan Daniels, *MacUser*, "Free MP3s," editorial.
19. Si Scott, Designersblock, 100% Design exhibition, *Love* posters.
20. Peter Field, *Pain Relief*, personal project.

21

22

Profile: Mr bingo

1

2

3

4

"The humor or the idea usually comes first, then making it aesthetically pleasing comes second."

Mr bingo has been working full-time in illustration for just three years, having spent the previous three, following his graduation, in a succession of dead-end jobs. "I worked in a show shop, a bank, and finally at a PR agency. The last job was so awful it made me more determined to succeed at something that I enjoy doing. It really spurred me on to find success as an illustrator," he admits.

1. *GQ* magazine, "Beer Goggles," editorial.
2. Faber & Faber, *The Book of General Ignorance*, book cover.
3. Platinum Asset Management, *Curious Investor Behaviour*, booklet.
4. More T Vicar, Prog Rock T-shirt design.

5

"It is the ordinary things that happen around me as much as the things in the news that influence my thinking. I like banal things, stupid things."

6

7

He set to work refining his approach and building up a client base, which now includes Oxfam, Carhartt, Converse, BBC, Nike, Orange, and Virgin. His secret to securing clients? "I find it so important to have constant communication with a client, so they know what they are going to get. That way, nobody ends up upset," he states.

When it comes to creative thinking, Mr bingo has a method for capturing ideas. "In the studio I write everything down on scraps of paper, when I travel it is always with a sketchbook, and I also keep a book in the bathroom. I started it five years ago and I'm currently on volume 8. It's a creative journal for collected thoughts while sitting on the toilet. A volume can only leave the bathroom once completed."

The studio may house the scraps of paper that record Mr bingo's ideas, but his most creative thinking occurs elsewhere. "I find it hard to come up with great ideas when I really try, or when I'm under pressure," he states. "I do, however, come up with a lot of good ideas when I'm in the bath, on a train, or in a pub. I hardly switch off and usually think about the work that I'm doing even when I'm on holiday. It is the ordinary things that happen around me as much as the things in the news that influence my thinking. I like banal things, stupid things," reflects Mr bingo. "I'm always watching people and listening to stuff that they say."

Mr bingo's straight-up, simple line-drawn illustrations provoke an immediate response in their audience: they deliver a

8

9

10

11

smile to the face with their honest humor and wit. In response to the question of how he views his strengths, bingo responds, "It takes a total commitment and dedication, loving what I do everyday, and being handy with a pen. Oh, and I'm good at talking money and smooching into magazines."

5.   Zeta Zanders, *Fat free*, promotional book.

6.   *GQ* magazine, "Gossiping Cow," editorial.

7.   Orange, Orange World, ad.

8.   *GQ* magazine, "Ozzy vs. China," editorial.

9.   *GQ* magazine, "12 Steps to the Crack House," editorial.

10. *GQ* magazine, "Licence to Ill," editorial.

11. The *Guardian*, "I Did it Mala-way," editorial.

Profile:
Adrian Johnson

1

2

"Ideas and concepts are fundamental to my working process. I guess it's the copy that's the bedrock for my ideas."

3

SAY YOUR PRAYERS.

Adrian Johnson is under pressure to complete his regular weekly slot illustrating a sports column written by comedian Russell Brand for the *Guardian* newspaper. Most weeks, Johnson has only an hour or so to conjure up his own witty take on Brand's copy and return a fully fledged illustration. "Ideas and concepts are fundamental to my working process," continues Johnson. "I guess it's the copy that's the bedrock for my ideas. I would like to say that my political viewpoints influence my thinking, but sadly, I think it's more often down to what makes me go 'oohh, that's daft, but looking good.' Time, of course is always a factor."

Based in London's Clerkenwell, just a stone's throw from both the *Guardian*'s offices and a lap-dancing club, Johnson shares studio space with three graphic designers, a moviemaker, a copywriter, and another illustrator. It's 10 years since Johnson graduated and began his life as an illustrator. "Sometimes it feels like much less, sometimes so much longer," he admits. Having moved out of London to reside in the countryside,

Johnson now commutes in. "I tend to rustle in about 10.00/11.00am, and then, after a few strong coffees and my daily perusal of www.evertonfc.com, I get stuck into a day's graft. I tend to finish around 8.00pm, though my workload recently has meant 13- and 14-hour days. When that happens I tend to hibernate at the weekends."

Asked to reflect upon his own practice as an illustrator he returns a brief, but typically witty artist's statement. "Adrian Johnson reads, thinks, draws, and does the color bit on a computer. It's hardly quantum physics." Johnson's humorous thinking and ideas are crucial to his illustrations, but he describes music as being the driving force behind how his work has developed. "When I was studying at art school I was really into the Mod scene, Northern Soul [two concurrent UK-based subcultures of the late 1960s/early 1970s, combining American soul and R'n'B music with European notions of street style and high fashion], and, of course, '60s culture in general," recalls Johnson from behind another double-shot latte. "It was during this period that I stumbled into the work of Paul Rand, Saul Steinberg, and Saul Bass. The *Pink Panther* movies in particular were an influence—everything from the opening credits to the soundtrack. It all had a profound impact on me as a boy. The idea of suggesting environments with abstract shape, color, or texture is something I've always been fascinated with."

Music's influence on Johnson remains strong. His iPod, hooked up to the studio speakers, is playing Mogwai. "I am partial to a bit of soft rock though," admits Johnson. "Unfortunately, the novelty of Def Leppard among my studio peers is always short-lived." Johnson's work has its own, distinct soundtrack playing in his mind. "I often imagine my work to have a xylophone-based sound, mixed in with a little Spanish horn and harpsichord." As the caffeine kicks in, Johnson's mind stops meandering, returns to his impending deadline, and he's straight back to his screen.

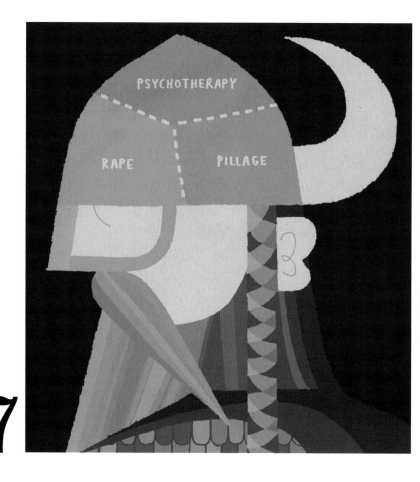

7

"Adrian Johnson reads, thinks, draws, and does the color bit on a computer. It's hardly quantum physics."

7. The *Guardian*, "Psychotherapy," editorial.
8. Vodafone, Turn fish-fingers into a Sunday roast, ad.

8

Profile: Pietari Posti

1

1. Trust Nobody Gallery, slip-mat artwork for Slipmad exhibition.
2. *Afisha* magazine, "Paul Verhoeven," editorial.

2

"If time allows, I like to sleep on a project and look at the piece with fresh eyes in the morning."

Pietari Posti has built an impressive editorial client list—*Time Out London*, *National Geographic*, *New Scientist*, *Dazed & Confused*, the *Guardian*, *The Times*—all within just 18 months. In 2005, following his graduation from the Lahti Institute of Art and Design in Finland, his home turf, he moved to Barcelona where his career really took off.

Reflecting upon his art and design education, Posti admits to being self-taught to a certain degree. "There is no proper education for illustrators in Finland. If you want to draw in school, basically you have

to choose between an education in graphic design or in fine art," he explains. "In school I learned to appreciate the whole field of design generally."

However, it was comic artists who fed Posti's imagination. Looking at children's comics, superhero strips, and later at more underground and adult comics, proved to be a huge inspiration throughout his childhood and education. It is not difficult to see their influences. Posti's work combines deft linework and a bold use of color. "I start by creating a really rough thumbnail sketch

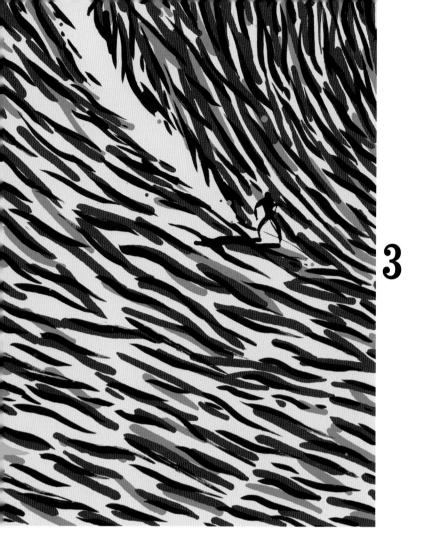

3

to figure out the composition. After that, I create a second one for more accurate lines and shapes, sometimes adding some color in Photoshop to help get my vision across to an art director." With approval from the client, Posti moves the process on. "I then scan and blow up the sketch, and print it out," he continues. "I trace the print out on a lightbox and then rescan the final linework at 600dpi, clean it up, add and erase if necessary, and finally add the color." The work isn't over though. "If time allows, I like to sleep on a project and look at the piece with fresh eyes in the morning," he adds. "It helps me see things I hadn't noticed the night before."

Despite the fastidious processes that Posti employs, his work also relies on creative thinking and clever ideas, and perhaps equally important is his sense that he is letting the viewer enter his own take on the world. "My illustrations," Posti reasons, "are about turning my ideas into flesh. It is about my imagination, the way I see the world, or the way I would like to see it, as well as my persona, my mood, my likes and dislikes …" Posti hopes his audience can relate to him through his image-making. "I am trying to make you understand me and feel what I'm feeling," Posti explains. "It is a form of communication, but sometimes it is more like a monologue than a conversation." Posti's images are so often beautiful glimpses into a place that we wish we existed in—they communicate a unique, timeless reflection of our memories.

Posti may have left many of his childhood memories in Finland, but he is constantly connected to his homeland while working. "I listen to a lot of radio via the web. Radio Helsinki is excellent!'

3. *Rojo* magazine, "Dream of Raymond Pettibon," editorial.
4. Hill & Knowlton, Finnish Presidency Guide, ad.
5. Environmental Super League, Practical Law, ad.
6. *American Way* magazine, "Giro d´Italia 1," editorial.
7. *New Scientist*, "Clocks," editorial.

4

"I am trying to make you understand me and feel what I'm feeling. It is a form of communication, but sometimes it is more like a monologue than a conversation."

5

6

7

Tutorial 3: Natsko Seki

Natsko Seki's eclectic images are often a mix of "found" elements, scanned drawings, collaged textures, and unique figures, all constructed with her own brand of wit and clever thinking.

Commissioned by *Elle Deco* magazine, Japanese illustrator, designer, and animator Natsko Seki created this image in response to the magazine's feature about the book *Not Buying It*. This book relates the life of the author and her partner following their decision to purchase nothing other than basic necessities for one year. The couple learnt exactly what they could and couldn't live without, and the simple pleasures of public libraries and parks.

1 Seki's concept was based around the idea of using shopping bags in a cityscape. As she explains, Seki wanted to create a street scene with "sad shopping-bag apartments and houses with just one building, in which the people who had quit shopping lived, happy and normal." She started by creating quick collages, scanning the elements, and laying them down very loosely at the start.

2 The next step for Seki was to print out her rough collage and hand-trace the image in order to submit the visual to the art director at the magazine. "Roughs of collages can often give the impression that they are half-finished work. Simple drawings are the best form for clients to see your first ideas," she explains.

3 Sometimes Seki will produce numerous visuals, but for this project she submitted three. Feedback from the client suggested that Seki look at drawing all of the buildings as shopping bags, and that the people in the street should all look happy and free—a marked contrast to the sad, colorless, and depressed-looking shopping-bag homes of her original idea.

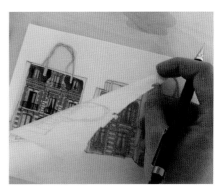

4 Sourcing reference material is important to getting the right look and feel for images. Seki researched a range of materials, including Japanese fashion magazines and books about British architecture. Using references to ensure the detailing within her drawings is correct is vital to Seki's working methods.

5 Combining elements from the outline drawings of the bags and the buildings was the next stage in creating the final artwork. Seki worked in Photoshop to bring together each of the elements. "These funny looking buildings excited me," she recalls.

6 Seki printed out the image on her studio ink-jet printer, and began tracing the image. "It's important to ensure that you draw to the scale at which the image will be reproduced. It is the only way to keep the pencil linework consistent within the image," she explains. "I always use a 0.5mm sharp pencil and lots of tracing paper."

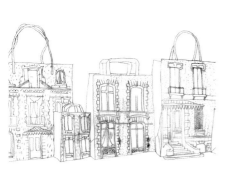

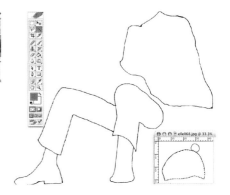

7 Leaving traces of the drawing process is key to Seki's approach. "I always try to leave the smudges when I scan—it looks more real. Strangely, adding extra marks and smudges gave the shabby, depressed buildings a more genuine feel."

8 Adding the human element was Seki's next task. She found an image of a man with an interesting posture, and used this as the starting point for the first character. To ensure that the image reflected a range of age-groups, Seki made hi-res scans of a youthful body and a middle-aged head.

9 Again Seki traced the image. "I didn't want to add fashionable details to his clothes," she says, "but I did draw him a hat to make him look good."

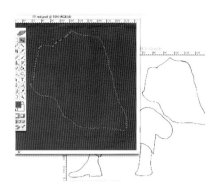

10 A key element of Seki's illustrations is her use of "found" textures. "I found this dirty red paper on a market stall," she explains. "It gave a much better texture than just filling in with the Paint Bucket in Photoshop." Using the Magic Wand she selected the character's jumper, dragged the selection onto the scanned red paper, then copied the selected shape.

11 With the jumper carefully pasted onto the man's body, Seki used the same process for his trousers, shoes, and hat. She then drew carefully around his face, hands, and newspaper with the Pen Tool, releasing them from the background.

12 Next, she color-altered each element of clothing in Photoshop by adjusting Brightness/Contrast, Hue/Saturation, and Curves. This basically means that any color combination can be created from the original scanned piece of red paper.

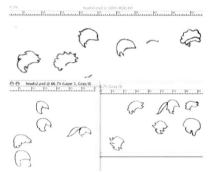

13 The image of the jumping girl went through the same process. Her hair was left blank at this stage, to be added as a drawn image later.

14 Each character was carefully created and applied to the image. Not sure how many figures to add, Seki worked on and added one at a time until she felt the image was working visually. The people in the shopping-bag buildings were colored black to suggest their depressing life.

15 Once all the characters were complete and in place, Seki printed the image and, using her 0.5mm sharp pencil, drew their hair onto tracing paper. "Hairstyles are quite important, and fun to draw. The style can really alter a personality. I often draw a number of styles for one person to see what works best."

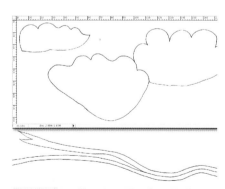

16 For additional elements Seki drew clouds and ribbons, scanned them, and added color using the same red-paper process.

17 The added extras included birds, a dog, and balloons. "They were either from the archive of photographs I have taken over the years, or the old magazines I collect," Seki notes.

18 Seki printed the final image in a number of colors. "It can take a long time to get the right balance and harmony between background and clothes," she admits. "The sky just seemed to work in green this time."

1. *PR Week*, "Cultural Leadership," editorial.
2. *Toshi Ni Sumu*, "Nice Flat," editorial.
3. Muji catolog, *MujiLife*, cover design.
4. The *Guardian*, *Family Forum* supplement, editorial.
5. Hankyu Department Stores, Chocolate Party, ad.

7

The Digit vs. the Digital

In one corner, fighting hard to retain the crown, digital technology; in the other, old-school, handcrafted image-making…

1 PICK ME

1. Richard Stow, *Blank* magazine, "Pick Me Helen," editorial.
2. David Sparshott, *Evening Post*, personal project.

Computers are worthless

"Computers are worthless. They can only give you answers." This was Pablo Picasso's reflection on the humble computer, albeit uttered long before the digital revolution was even a sparkle in the eyes of Mr Gates or Mr Jobs. Picasso's death in 1973 ensured that he would play no part in the birth of digital art, but his sentiment is one that captures the current zeitgeist for turning off and tuning out of hours in front of the screen.

In the twenty-first century, owning and using a computer is expected. In the life of the average twenty-something, the beige box of tricks has been part of the furniture. For this generation of designers, illustrators, and image-makers, there is a brave new world of old technologies and traditional working methods to discover.

Illustrators and designers growing up in the 1990s were ensured access to a computer from the cradle to the classroom. Staring at

a screen became the norm. If you weren't glued to Pong and Pac-Man on a PC, battling Sonic on a Sega, or getting jiggy with Mario on a Game Boy, you were attempting to create images with MacPaint or PixelPaint, exploring the newfangled World Wide Web, or sending a text on your Nokia 3210. The keyboard and screen reigned supreme. It was really no wonder that the digital had such a stranglehold on image-making—here was the future, in the here and now.

But, as Picasso had envisaged, the beige box, now more commonly a flat-screen monitor, provided only the answers. Crisp, digital solutions and a fashion for super-slick, vector-traced, what-you-see-is-what-you-get images has emerged in recent years. In providing more answers than questions, the computer has removed any element of chance. In the crop of recent digital imagery there has been little room for risk, for failure, and, more importantly, for the hand of the artist to shine through. For a while, software had taken over. Originality and individualism had become far less important than cool control over a vector curve.

3. Adam Hayes, Design Interactions at the RCA, flyer.
4. Kerry Roper, Nike Air Jordan T-shirt design.
5. Peter James Field, *NatWest Private Banking Magazine*, "Columnists," editorial.
6. Tom Cornfoot, *Fact* magazine, "Typical Girls," editorial.

Innovation and mediocrity

It was Milton Glaser, designer of one of the world's most recognizable logos, **I♥NY**, who once stated, "Computers are to design as microwaves are to cooking." The man had a point. Heating TV dinners rather than cooking with fresh ingredients can leave the palette craving new tastes and experiences. Serving up mediocre and mundane dishes day after day isn't good for the soul, but experimentation is the spice of life.

Kerry Roper, who has worked on projects for Nike and Snickers, combines illustration, photography, and typography within his images and sees experimentation as the way forward. "I have always enjoyed experimenting with imagery. When an image is created by hand, I think it becomes more personal—unique." Roper believes in a hands-on attitude. "I first used Deluxe Paint on the Commodore Amiga back in 1989. It wasn't until around 1994 that I started using a Mac and Photoshop. Even then I was very hands-on. I created collages by experimenting with the photocopier and Omnichrom machines." These transferred color from a film sheet to a black-and-white photocopy—very hi-tech at the time.

From hi-tech to low-fi

Roper is philosophical about the reasons behind this gradual shift back to more hands-on working techniques. "The industry tends to be led by visual trends. A while back there was a glut of vector- and computer-generated imagery, and it all ended up looking so very similar." Craig Atkinson adds his own thoughts as to why the change has occurred. "I just think that people have realized the computer is a valuable tool, but hands are more valuable," he states. Atkinson, an artist and illustrator with over 10 years of exhibiting under his belt, continues. "Everything was just so slick for a while; it was all so process-led. I think it led straight up a blind alley, and as the process itself couldn't change, it was the artist who needed to initiate it. The only real way out has been a radical move toward the opposite—the low-fi."

Holly Wales, who by her own admission "works nonstop," combines her working methods. "I think, for me, it was natural to find a hands-on approach to go alongside my digital work, which," she states, "always seemed to be slightly unsatisfying by itself." Wales, just over a year since graduating, has

already chalked up an impressive client list that includes the *Independent*, *The Illustrated Ape* magazine, and the Art Directors Club of Germany. "My dad is a graphic designer and used to build his own robots and computers, so I grew up alongside them," she states. But her own take on the recent surge in a more crafts-based approach to image-making reflects her sense of humor rather than a genuine, considered, and rational argument. The return is probably because, "staring at a computer screen for too long is bad and leads to dangerous activities such as mail-order brides and blindness." Quite.

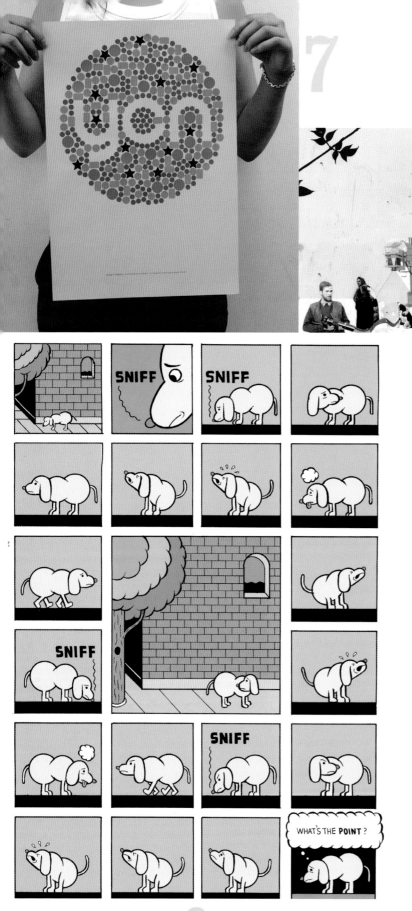

We shape our tools

Marshall McLuhan, the visionary who coined the phrase "the Global Village" in his seminal book *The Medium is the Massage*, once said, "We become what we behold. We shape our tools and then our tools shape us." In recent years our digital tools have provided us with seemingly endless options for drawing and painting tools, with a vast array of pens and brushes that take us further and further away from the origins of the physical instruments. As more illustrators and designers go back to basics, the tendency to be shaped by our technology has started to be bucked. Many are resisting the pull of technology and fighting back.

"I always carry a sketchbook," states Craig Atkinson. "That's where a lot of my ideas start. I draw a lot, just for myself." Atkinson admits to "fairly basic working methods," and lists his tools and techniques of choice. "Pen, pencil, paper, and collage. I'll use the computer sometimes just to tidy something up a little, sometimes for trying layers and colors within an image." His work is also influenced by ideas and themes. "I like to draw situations and places that I have never been in or to," he offers. "I made a book for a show at the Junc Gallery in LA about what it's like to live in LA. I've never even been there so it was just based on things that I've heard or imagine about the city." Not the easiest or the most normal of working methods, but one that has snared projects from the likes of *The New York Times*, *Esquire* magazine, and Orange.

7. Melvin Galapon, YCN, YCN Award commendation certificates.
8. Tez Humphreys, *Encore* magazine, "Dog Trap," editorial.
9. Andy Rementer, *Trevopolis*, personal project.
10. Craig Atkinson, *Sketchbook*, personal project.
11. Paul Burgess, *Burning Spear*, personal project.

My niece can draw better than you

In the search for originality, many artists challenge their own drawing techniques by using tools in innovative ways, allowing them to work at evolving new styles and means of expression. Holly Wales, from her studio in east London, explains. "I'm very interested in traditional design considerations like line, composition, and balance. They usually play a big part in shaping my images." However, as Wales elaborates, she likes "to hold pens in different hands—left, right, both— to get different results. A friend recently bought me a foot-long pencil. It has really freed my drawing up," she admits. Reactions to her work, despite a growing client base, include: "My niece can draw better than you," and "Why don't you hire a six-year-old to do it for you?" These just make Wales more determined. "Oh, I just see it as a reason to create more work," she states in a matter-of-fact, couldn't-give-a-darn kind of way.

"My grandmother likes my work and that makes me feel good," admits Andy Rementer. "I do all my drawing and lettering the old-fashioned way; at the drawing table." Rementer was born in New Jersey, educated in Philadelphia, and, following a career in NYC working at MTV and TeamHeavy, is now living and working in Italy. He admits to a lifelong passion for his work saying, "I've always been a doodler." With a body of work that incorporates a weekly cartoon strip, "Techno Tuesday," published in print and online, and projects such as the Teach Me

10

festival for Studio Camuffo, Rementer has a certain way with a pencil. "The benefit of doing everything by hand," he explains, "is that one day, if all the computers in the world break down … I'll still have something genuine and original to offer." Rementer may sound like he's joking, but his dark view of technology and the future is one that is shared by others.

Paul Burgess, collage artist, illustrator, and designer with a 20-year back catalog, agrees with Rementer. "The benefits of working in the way I do? I never get bored, and if my computer goes down I'm always OK!" Burgess is keen to see a return to a crafts-based approach from a wider perspective. "What is happening," he offers, "goes hand in hand with what's happening in music. There is a big return to loud guitar bands right now. As technology increases in the world, so people want to simplify their lives. They don't want to be suffocated by it."

11

The digit vs. the digital

Digital technology may have fallen out of favor of late, but most designers and artists agree it still plays a vital role—it is now the medium that pulls together every handcraft discipline and, alongside the scanner and the digital camera, acts as the artist's desktop, canvas, drawing board, and darkroom. "It seems that illustrators have settled down to using the computer as a tool," explains Corinna Radcliffe, herself inspired by Indian art, Victorian decoration, Japanese wood blocks, and 1960s poster art. "The computer is no longer an exclusive way of working," she continues. "Handcraft techniques now provide more of the basis of the work being created." Radcliffe's own work blends both hand-drawn and collaged elements. "I've always begun images by hand: it allows my personal style to come through," she explains. "The computer enables me to turn often quite simple sketches into more complex compositions and images, and allows me to color them in various ways using gradients and outlines impossible by hand."

12. Richard Stow, *Blank* magazine, "Cat and Mouse," editorial.

13. Naja Conrad-Hansen, Purenomade, ad.

14. Tez Humphreys, *Blowback* magazine, "Supreme Being," editorial.

15

mie Oliver.

16

17

18

15. Neil McFarland, Jaguar Shoes, *House Fire*, Papercuts exhibition piece.

16. Patrick Morgan, *Waitrose Food Illustrated* magazine, "Jamie Oliver," editorial.

17. Neil McFarland, *See The Wood*, personal project.

18. Fiodor Sumkin, *Rock Out, F$!@ Glam!*, personal project.

19

Finding a method for combining the analogue and the digital while retaining a unique personal visual language is now top of the agenda for those embarking upon a creatively fruitful pathway. "I'm always keen to keep some of the irregularities and my own personal drawing style that comes through when working by hand, the computer just gives me greater options," explains Radcliffe. "I think," adds Craig Atkinson, "that my self-taught approach to working on the computer helps my work not look too slick, which I like. Also, I wouldn't want the digital to overshadow the analogue as far as my working methods are concerned."

Andy Rementer, working in Italy, muses, "Perhaps artists just became bored staring at computer screens all day, or perhaps it's just another trend."

20

19. Corinna Radcliffe, *Jungle*, Giclee Print, exhibition piece.

20. Corinna Radcliffe, *Kremlin*, personal project.

21. Alex Williamson, *Sunday Times*, "Stephen King," editorial.

22. Alex Williamson, *Catalog 1*, personal project.

23. Hennie Haworth, *Plan B Magazine*, "Matmos," editorial.

24. Alex Robbins, *Man's Best Friend*, personal project.

25. Fiodor Sumkin, *Chinese New Year Dragon*, personal project.

1

2

"My current output is the result of a year of fine-tuning and readjusting," admits Holly Wales. "It is based on things I'm interested in, and materials I like to work with. If I have a success with an experiment, I'll work at it more and more until it becomes second nature."

"I'd spent the past five years working from home," begins Wales. "Finally, the pressures of washing up after everyone else, and eating five bowls of cereal every day became too much," she adds.

Out of college for just two years, Wales admits there is much to discover. "I share the studio with a menswear designer and another illustrator. We have great big windows and a brilliant library," Wales explains. "I still have so much to learn that being around other people is great." For Wales, a career in illustration was almost predestined.

"My parents had a big influence. As designers they would always encourage me to draw at all times, but more crucially they made me think about things. I don't think any profession thinks more," offers Wales, with a note of seriousness in her voice that makes it a convincing statement.

Mixing media and experimentation has become a constant theme in Wales' work. "I usually pass the time carving Byzantine-style sculptures," she confesses with a smile on her face. "When I feel I've done enough of that I just draw, scan, edit, print, draw,

1. YCN, *Utopia*, ad.
2. *Little Whilte Lies*, "Parker Posey," editorial.

trace, scan, print..." Her relationship with technology started when she young. "I got my first Apple Mac aged 11," Wales recalls. "I'd use Adobe PageMaker to redesign all of the junk mail that came through the post. I have no idea why. For kicks maybe!" she jokes.

Wales' approach does have a serious side. "I am very interested in traditional design elements like line, composition, and balance," she explains. "I love the process of putting all of the ideas together and reaching that moment when it starts to look right." With a growing client list, Wales has only recently started to think about dividing her time between commercial and self-initiated projects. "I do think that personal projects are a really important aspect of being creative," she states. "It helps to set yourself up for the future, if you don't let style or fashion get in the way too much."

Maintaining a tough work ethic comes naturally to Wales. She admits to having to force herself to take holidays and even leave the studio every day before cabin fever sets in. "I'm always trying to cram too much in. I am both hindered and encouraged in equal measures by wanting to do everything right now!" she passionately exlaims.

"I got my first Apple Mac aged 11," Wales recalls. "I'd use Adobe PageMaker to redesign all of the junk mail that came through the post. I have no idea why."

3

4

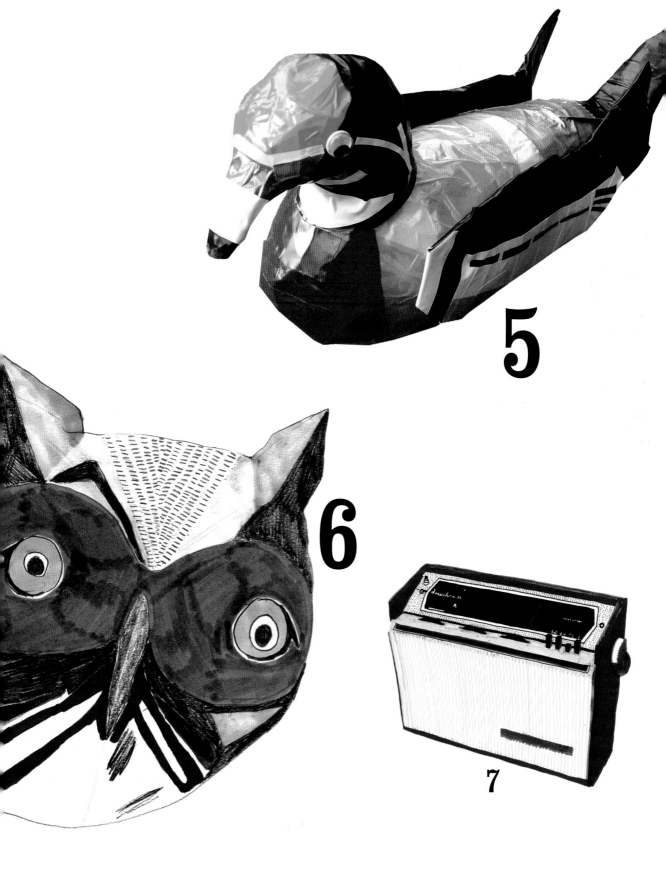

5

6

7

3. *Little White Lies*, "Big sandwich," edtorial.
4. *Plan B Magazine*, "Pulp rerelease," editorial.
5. Sellotape duck, personal project.
6. Stereohype, "Owl," for online fashion boutique.
7. *Plan B Magazine*, "Radio," editorial.

Profile: Asako Masunouchi

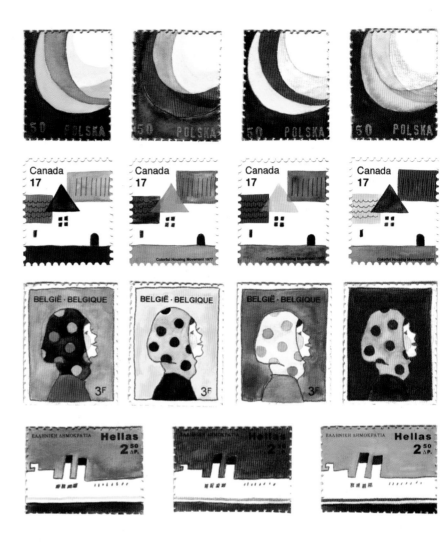

1

"My illustrations are momentary images from everyday life, which are sometimes melancholy, nostalgic, and humorous," explains Asako Masunouchi from her studio near Tokyo.

There is a timeless beauty to Masunouchi's work. Her illustrations and animations are a blend of well-considered, yet simple hand-drawn linework brought to life with muted pastels. Beautiful figures inhabit her drawings. They recall an era inspired by 1960s fashion, of childhood memories and a simpler time.

The tools of Masunouchi's craft are set out in her well-organized studio: a sketchbook, color pencils, and an Apple Mac laptop are on the desk beneath her window. This window overlooks her supermarket, a practice area for a Ground Self Defense Force, and a small deserted park—all aspects of the everyday that feed her imagination.

Masunouchi's studio hi-fi plays through the back catalog of the Beatles while she works on a new series of editorial illustrations. Her influences line the shelves, and the walls—photographs, postcards, toys, magazines, and books are ordered neatly. Affixed to the wall next to her workspace, a Post-It® to-do list documents the tasks ahead. Masunouchi admits to a working process that relies on an impending deadline. "I have a sketchbook that I use to write thoughts in, but I need some pressure. To make these ideas a reality, I need labored consideration."

2

The working day for Masunouchi can easily last 12 hours or more. "I tend to work from midday to midnight on weekdays," she explains, "and often work at the weekends too." Is it her prolific output that demands these hours, or does creating such seemingly simple images just take time? "I make anything from 10 to 20 sketches before starting on roughs for the client," offers Masunouchi. "I'll then choose a few to show, and from that stage to the final artwork, I'll maybe create another couple of sketches." This confirms that mastering the art of simplicity and economy of visual information can be a painstaking task.

Masunouchi claims her weakness to be time management, despite her diligence and the organized structure of her working week. She also admits to being easily upset. When starting out, she took a full-time job at a design studio, but left after just one week because she was asked to make illustrations that the company's art director had originally wanted another illustrator to create. "Because of factors that included time and economics, I had to deform my drawings into somebody else's," she sighs. It was not a proud moment in her career, but it did help her establish strict work criteria. "I don't cling to a style. I have various ways of making work."

Masunouchi has created work for clients that include publishers Penguin, Faber & Faber, and Bloomsbury in the UK; and Kadokawa Shoten, Kodansha, and NHK in Japan. With the future looking increasingly bright for Masunouchi, it would appear that the 12-hour day may not be quite long enough.

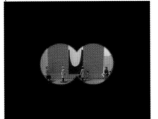
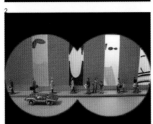
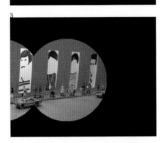
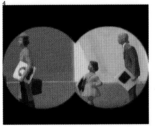

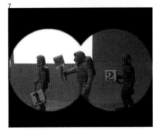

3

1. Bijutsu Shuppan-sha, *Coloring Stamps*, promotion.
2. Vue Sur La Ville, *Avril*, calendar.
3. Le Book, *Connections*, promotion.
4. Hamish Hamilton/Penguin, *Japanese for Travellers*, book.

4

5

"I make anything from 10 to 20 sketches before starting on roughs for the client," offers Masunouchi. "I'll then choose a few to show, and from that stage to the final artwork, I'll maybe create another couple of sketches."

6

1. Début Art, *Poem*, promotion.
2. Début Art, *Profile*, exhibition piece.

Oliver Hydes, passionate about the art of the illustrator, raises an interesting point. With the fickle fashion of constantly searching for the "next big thing," illustration may, for a short while, have forgotten its roots. The art of picture-making and storytelling was so easily lost as the floodgates of digital image-making opened. For many, the means of working digitally were more important than content and traditional handcrafting skills.

But make no mistake; Hydes is no Luddite when it comes to his craft. "I tend not to create too many sketches before embarking upon an artwork," he admits. "I usually compose various elements of an image on the computer and print that out as a rough, a visual guide, and then complete the image by hand." It all sounds so simple, but this description of the final aspect of his working process is something of an understatement.

Hydes often works on huge sheets of paper, by hand, with felt-tip pens. Tools not known for their ability to stand the test of time, they bleed, they run dry, and they are very unforgiving. If you make a mistake, it will show. "I use them on a large scale," Hydes explains, "as I'm particularly interested in the *process* of creating an image. I like being able to see the build-up of the image, and the labor involved. I do enjoy being able to see that an image has been crafted using skill and ingenuity."

Along with his interest in the traditional uses of color, shape, and formats in image-making, Hydes also lists "simplicity and complexity, typography and numbers, outsider artists, and girlfriend's critical eye" as driving factors in his work.

3. *Disorder* magazine, *RedHotChiliPeppers*, promotion.
4. noWax, *Number 11*, promotion.
5. FunkyGandhi, P is for Peace T-shirt design.
6. *SEED* magazine, "Brain Training," editorial.

His images do take a certain raw determination and, although they involve a time-consuming process, that doesn't faze Hydes. "I've always produced artwork, and I've always held exhibitions of my work—ever since leaving school—so it is a natural process to do art and design for a living. Nothing really interests me as much as image-making. It's an extension of yourself and your thoughts. I think, if it is in you, it is simply something that you have to do."

Hydes divides his time between commercial projects and self-initiated work and exhibitions in a 60:40 ratio. His clients include Channel 4 TV, Visit London, and FunkyGandhi in the UK, along with *SEED* magazine in the US. His list of recent exhibitions is equally impressive, but Hydes still enjoys—or endures, depending on his frame of mind—a working process that keeps him alert. "I've never had anything go horribly wrong with an artwork, but at some stage during any new piece of work, I'll start to feel that it could go wrong at any point. I always have a period of self-doubt about how it is looking, but I know if I stick it out, it will all eventually come together." It is a philosophy that has born witness to the creation of some remarkable artworks, and is one that looks set to continue his career trajectory onward and upward.

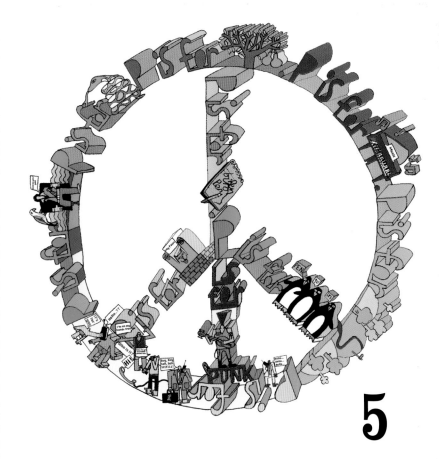

5

6

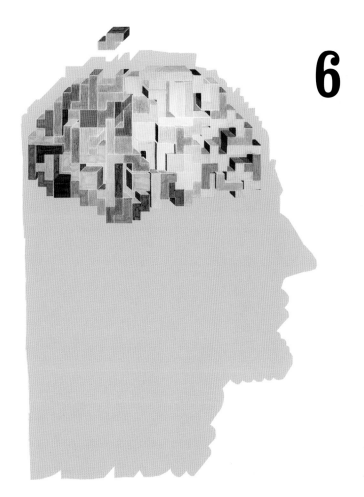

"At some stage during any new piece of work, I'll start to feel that it could go wrong at any point. I always have a period of self-doubt about how it is looking, but I know if I stick it out, it will all eventually come together."

Case Study:
The All-Service Studio

1

2

3

4

Breaking out of the traditional confines of illustration, Matt Wingfield Studio crosses boundaries and borders to create work for clients that span a variety of media.

Matt Wingfield is taking delivery of three pallets of Mirri-Board, heavy card sheets finished in silver. He'll be screen printing onto both sides of this to create 1,700 boards for display in Monsoon's fashion retail stores. The project, based loosely on the theme of Havana, Cuba, is for the menswear division of Monsoon. "The core of what we do is designing and making," explains Wingfield. "Basically we offer a design service that is carried right through to the making of the graphic for the client."

Wingfield stands in his new studio, a converted warehouse that now houses his screen-printing and lamination equipment. "We're constantly working on a range of projects, many quite unlike anything we've done before." Wingfield was the first student

on his course to make the transition from graphics and illustration to textiles. It is perhaps his apparent ease in breaking boundaries that has led him to his current core business—working with a crop of fashion retail clients, creating graphic solutions for their in-store and window promotions. "I'm a visual cowboy," he admits. "I'm like a bad builder: I go in, get the brief, and create work that is flippant and disposable. I have only been 'in-trend' once or twice in the last 10 years! Being 'off-trend' most of the time means that I just get to do what I like doing. I have to keep being creative. I try to create work that interests me and hopefully that interests my clients…" It certainly does more than just interest his clients—an impressive list that includes

> **"I'm a visual cowboy," he admits. "I'm like a bad builder: I go in, get the brief, and create work that is flippant and disposable. I have only been 'in-trend' once or twice in the last 10 years!"**

Topshop, Ted Baker, and Harvey Nichols, where he worked as window designer. Matt Wingfield Studio (MWS) might concentrate much of its time working for street-label fashion stores, but a good part of its portfolio has been built up working for a range of media. Wingfield works as an illustrator, creating images for many magazines and publications. He has also designed, manufactured, and promoted his own range of disposable cardboard furniture. His limited-edition, screen-printed flatpack coffee tables captured the attention of the design press when launched in 1998. Named Affordable Luxury, the whole idea of the range, Wingfield explains, "was to produce something that was environmentally sound, yet didn't feel apologetic. I wanted the pieces to have real personality." And they certainly have bags of that.

So 10 years after graduation, where next for Matt Wingfield? "I want to retain that handmade feel in my work, but maybe make it a little more serious and grown-up." It is unlikely that the output from MWS will lose its quirkiness and originality though.

1. ZeegenRush, self-portrait, agency promotion.
2. Gallery Five, gift-wrap design.
3. Warner Fabrics, catwalk show promotion.
4. *Stacking Fruit Boxes*, personal project.
5. MWS studio and inspiration wall.
6. Flat-pack mannequin, personal project.
7. MWS studio, Matt's favorite chair.
8. MWS studio wall.
9. MWS studio's vinyl cutting area.
10. Harvey Nichols, print design.
11. MWS main studio.
12. Monsoon Menswear, window display and fabric label.

8

Tutorial 4: Matt Wingfield Studio

SLEEPING BAG

FEATURES
- **Filling:** 200 g/m2 hollowfibre
- **Shell:** 80% polyester / 20% cotton
- **Lining:** 80% polyester / 20% cotton
- **Build:** single layer, vertical 's' quilt

CAMPING   2 SEASON   200 X 95 X 95 cm

Matt Wingfield Studio (MWS) combines both traditional and digital image-creation techniques with reproduction methods that are very hands-on. Using in-house facilities, MWS demonstrates its approach to a recent retail project.

Matt Wingfield Studio was commissioned by the fashion retailer Oasis to create the branding for a summer in-store promotion entitled "Gone Camping." MWS wins many projects because of its quirky, unorthodox, and very hands-on approach to design. It is often viewed as the very antithesis of the one-size-fits-all approach to retail design. For this aspect of the project, MWS created a door ticket to be used as a hanging promotional device.

1 Designed, crafted, and printed in-house, the project needed a very handcrafted feel—an MWS specialty and fundamental to its approach. The first aspect of the project was to construct the base layer for the image. Pieces of wood were cut with a handsaw, then prepared by removing all loose chippings and splinters.

2 Next the wood was fixed to double-wall corrugated cardboard. Each piece was stapled to a base, leaving gaps and edges to create the handcrafted feel. Four separate artworks were created at this stage to allow for some degree of flexibility and experimentation.

3 A paint ground was applied to each of the four base artworks using a large household paintbrush. It was important to create a textural feel, and for each ground to be different.

4 With the grounds dry, Wingfield set about adding further texture and depth by scraping, overpainting, and spraying. The aim was to create a weathered or distressed effect as the final pieces need to look and feel as authentic as possible.

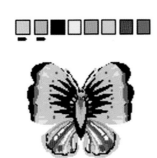

5 Working from an original textile design—a small detail on a fabric supplied by Oasis at the start of the project—Wingfield scanned a butterfly image, color-coded each constituent color, and prepared to redesign and reconfigure the image to add a handcrafted, low-tech feel.

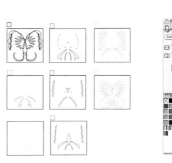

6 Using a bespoke software application, Wingfield then separated the artwork into eight distinct colors. This process worked in a very similar way to the creation of screen-print separations.

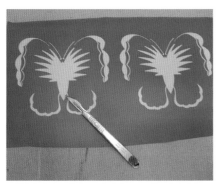

7 The artworked digital file was then plotted onto vinyl, using a cutter to create eight separate self-adhesive masks. Next, all the areas to which paint was to be applied were removed to create stencils through which color could be added to build up the image in stages.

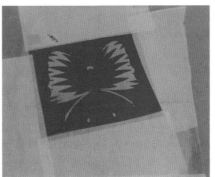

8 Using temporary registration marks, Wingfield carefully applied his first mask to the base board.

9 He began the coloring process by spraying through the vinyl stencils with aerosol paints, using a well-ventilated part of his studio and wearing a face mask to protect against fumes.

10 As layers of color were applied, the image started to take shape. Each stencil allowed more detail to be added. Decisions regarding the exact use and tone of color could change, which allowed for experimentation throughout the process. Much of the MWS approach is down to trial and error. "I like to allow for mistakes," Wingfield explains.

11 Wingfield works swiftly and succinctly, but is careful to allow happy accidents to occur. Sometimes a slight imperfection in registration or the quantity of paint applied helps to give the final image a less designed feel and more of the individuality needed in the project.

12 A closeup of one of the four artworks shows the detail, looseness, and imperfections that Wingfield works hard to achieve.

13 Happy with the execution at this point, Wingfield begins researching type treatments that will suit the overall look and feel. An interesting aspect of MWS design is that it often creates one-off typefaces for special projects. This font was created for Oasis projects.

14 Applying the font was the next step. The overall concept for the promotion was about summer, camping, and going to festivals. The type treatment needed to reflect these activities.

15 As for the image, Wingfield created a self-adhesive mask, removing the sticker from any areas to which paint was to be applied. While this process isn't complicated, it is all too easy to make mistakes, so careful attention was required.

16 Next, the typographic element was applied to separate artworks and butterfly graphics. It was important to provide numerous final artworks to give the client flexibility in applying it to a range of point-of-sale items.

17 With the illustration, type treatment, and overall look and feel complete, the final artwork was shot with a high-format digital camera. Once the image was digitized, any unrequired imperfections were removed, and the artwork was sent to Oasis for reproduction.

18 While MWS often design and print in-house, this project required a large-volume print run and reproduction onto a range of items. Despite the use of modern print techniques, the low-tech nature of the image creation remained clearly defined in this door ticket application.

1. Harvey Nichols, Scribble Sale window display.
2. Harvey Nichols, Curiosty Shop window display.
3. *Like a bird*, personal project.
4. 100% Design, Honolulu cardboard coffee table.

8

Where Fashion and Music Collide

Once, not such a long time ago, new trends in music and fashion emerged from the street.

2

Rock and roll

Street culture was once a rapidly changing affair. The first music created by and for teenagers—rock and roll—gave rise to the teddy boys of the 1950s and evolved into a constantly changing musical landscape that inspired new sounds and new styles: the mods, beatniks, and hippies of the 1960s; the skinheads, punks, and new romantics of the 1970s; and beyond. These lively youth movements were energized by a constant need for reinvention.

Music and fashion once seemed intertwined. Neither one existed, at least at street level, without the other. Both were vital aspects of each new subculture; both helped define a nation's youth as teenagers struggled to find their own identity. It could be argued that both the teenage and youth cultures were born in the US. Rock and roll was a resolutely American invention, although quickly absorbed and rethought by teens throughout the West.

"It could be argued that both the teenage and youth cultures were born in the US. Rock and roll was a resolutely American invention, although quickly absorbed and rethought by teens throughout the West."

1. Eleanor Grosch, Death Cab For Cutie, *Beaver*, concert poster.
2. Richard Ardagh, Paul Smith, T-shirt designs.
3. Karoly Kiralyfalvi, Logikwear, Mr. Wizard, T-shirt design.

3

Youth rebellion

The 1960s, 1970s, and 1980s were times of changing street culture, fueled by the simple act of youthful rebellion against authority, politics, and the older generation. Music was raw, honest, and powerful, as were the fashions that followed the sounds, emerging from council rather than fashion houses. This was a time before marketing and PR reigned supreme, before big corporations fully understood how to capitalize on subcultures and sell them back to the youth. This was a time when genres clashed, when street culture could evolve and mutate away from the glare of commercial pressure.

Design and illustration also played its part in defining this culture. The record sleeves of each decade captured a look and feel; they established a graphic identity for each movement. Consider Peter Blake's legendary *Sgt. Pepper's* sleeve for the Beatles, the surreal and dreamlike images created by Hypgnosis for Pink Floyd, Rick Griffin's psychedelic artwork for The Grateful Dead's *Aoxomoxoa*, Jamie Reid's raw, cut-and-paste mayhem for the Sex Pistols, and Peter Saville's timeless work for Joy Division.

4

5

"Music was raw, honest, and powerful, as were the fashions that followed the sounds, emerging from council rather than fashion houses."

4. Ryu Itadani, Higashi Mejiro Project (Tokyo), *Ginkgo*, exhibition piece.
5. Hennie Haworth, *Plan B Magazine*, "Electrelane," editorial.

HESSENMOB

HESSENMOB IS SKATEBOARDING. SKATEBOARDING IS CREATIVITY.

7

Art-school angst

Many illustrators grew up with a passion for music and fashion, often introduced to an eclectic mix of both through the tastes of their parents. For many, emerging from art school and going on to work across the fashion and music industries would appear a seamless transition. Music was an integral aspect of the art-school experience and art-school studios were catalysts for new styles, places where fashion was seen as something to be exploited and explored. Art students had, and still have, their own approach to looking good.

Marine recreates her own art-school ambience in her studio. "The music is always on in my studio," she states simply. Not only is her "love for music" the inspiration for her images, she also describes her working methods as including "lots of music." Clearly then, it plays a vital role in the creation of Marine's illustrations, and she acknowledges that many of her favorite clients have been involved in music design.

8

6.   MWM Graphics, *Vector Funk 2*, postcard book, personal project.

7.   Karoly Kiralyfalvi, Hessenmob Skateboards, *Creativity*, promotional poster.

8.   Marine, *Amelia's Magazine*, "The Pipettes," editorial.

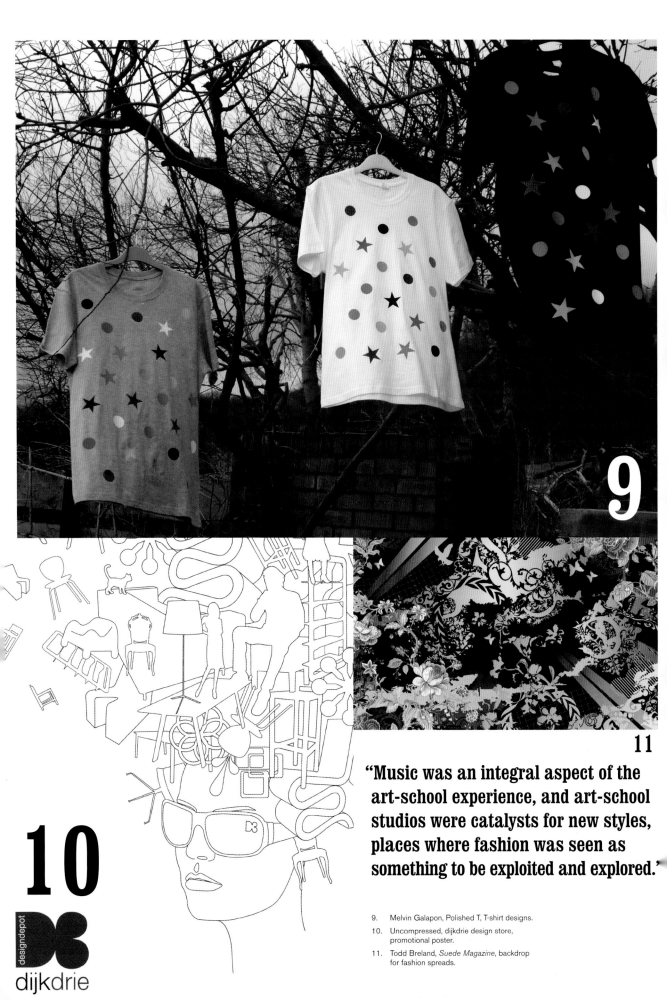

9

10

11

"Music was an integral aspect of the
art-school experience, and art-school
studios were catalysts for new styles,
places where fashion was seen as
something to be exploited and explored."

9. Melvin Galapon, Polished T, T-shirt designs.

10. Uncompressed, dijkdrie design store,
promotional poster.

11. Todd Breland, *Suede Magazine*, backdrop
for fashion spreads.

designdepot
dijkdrie

12

From free posters to company ownership

Eleanor Grolsh, originally trained in Fine Art at the University of South Florida and now working out of Philadelphia, USA, also found a way into graphic design and illustration through music. She started out designing gig posters, free of charge, for local bands, record companies, gig venues, and promoters as a way of building a portfolio. She also posted these on gigposters.com, a website dedicated to showcasing the best of the genre. It was a business approach that reaped rewards. Grolsh went from unpaid projects to running her own, successful design business within just a few short years.

Her work on music-related projects soon led to fully paid commissions in other key areas, from limited-edition prints, fashion, home furnishings, and gifts, to wallets, badges, and bags. Grolsh had begun to create her own brand. In 2003, she launched her company PushMePullYou. Working out of the basement of her studio, she screen prints much of her output by hand. Hard work and limitless energy and creativity have kept Grolsh on track. "I get an idea and work on it right away, while it is still fresh in my mind. If I wait too long, I don't get the same rush, and the process isn't as enjoyable."

13

12. Peter Nencini, Channel 4, Whatever, set-design graphics.
13. Eleanor Grosch, Keds, Owl, fabric design.

From music to fashion

For Grolsh the move from music to fashion wasn't problematic. She entered a collaboration with US shoe manufacturer Keds to create what she describes as "the cutest shoes around." Keds, established in 1916, was one of the first national athletic and lifestyle footwear brands, and in recent years has become known for shoes created with outside designers and illustrators. It is evident that the simple graphic, yet quirky images Eleanor Grolsch creates have found favor across the board.

Still in the US, but this time in New York City, Todd Alan Breland, working under the name IMNY, runs his studio on Ludlow Street on the Lower East Side. "I grew up in Virginia Beach, and I've been drawing and painting since I was a young child," he states, "taking art classes in and out of school and working my way up through college, where I finished up with a Bachelor degree in graphic design." With a client base that spans the US and takes in Paris, Tokyo, and London, it is clear that IMNY is in demand. Work for independent labels Nitro Records and Stillborn Records has been supplemented with projects for the likes of the Universal Music Group. On top of this, numerous fashion and style magazines, including *Nylon* and *Suede*, have commissioned IMNY's fashion-related work.

IMNY launched in 2004 and the studio started to gather momentum immediately, becoming recognized for a style and way of working that often encompasses a complex approach, building up layers of photographic and vector images. However, despite the richness of the work, there are times when IMNY feels directionless and uninspired. "I think I can speak for most artists," he states honestly, "in saying that when you're feeling creative you have to go with it. It's hard to put time on creativity. Some days I wake up and feel like I've stumbled into a whole new universe; I feel innovative and I'm all over the place. Other days I can stare at a blank canvas or mess around for hours and not feel the least bit inspired or motivated." However, IMNY continues to find inspiration for work, and commissions keep coming. He has just completed a project for Coca-Cola.

14

14. Joe McLaren, The Lodge: *Noose*, album cover.
15. Naja Conrad-Hansen, *Dance Floor Monkeys*, personal project.
16. Christian Montenegro, Levi's Argentina, Muertitos, ad.

15

With a method of working that can best be described as eclectic, Conrad Hansen's practice, in her own words, "embraces illustration, painting, graphic design, building fashion concepts, making silk-screen prints, and definitely more."

16

A passion for style and fashion

Naja Conrad-Hansen, who runs Meannorth, describes herself as an "illustrator/designer with a passion for style and fashion." Born to a Finnish mother and Danish father, she has lived in Finland, Greece, and Egypt. She now lives and works in Copenhagen, Denmark, but with agents representing her work in London, Berlin, and Milan, she has been making a name for herself much further afield.

Conrad-Hansen's prolific output belies her relatively recent entrance into the world of design and illustration. Meannorth has only been trading since her graduation in 2003. With five years of design training, following two years of fine-art education, her background also played a part in shaping her destiny as a designer and illustrator—her mother is a painter and her grandfather worked as a graphic designer at a time when billboards were still painted by hand.

With a method of working that can best be described as eclectic, Conrad-Hansen's practice, in her own words, "embraces illustration, painting, graphic design, building fashion concepts, making silk-screen prints, and definitely more." She admits that her inspirations come from "the worlds of fashion, hard-core music, and traditional art and design," and looks for her work to "find some untouched areas of the mind, and to stimulate the eye and the imagination."

Meannorth's creative output may not be typical of design and illustration studios—her style draws on a graphic language of sharp, in-your-face, punchy drawings, with patterns, colors, and letterforms that make her work unique—but a long list of clients keen for the Meannorth ethos to rub off have been utilizing her talents. Virgin; *Dazed & Confused*; *Rojo* magazine; US band Ministry; and noWax, the MP3 DJ club, have all commissioned works, and the trend doesn't look to be slowing up any time soon.

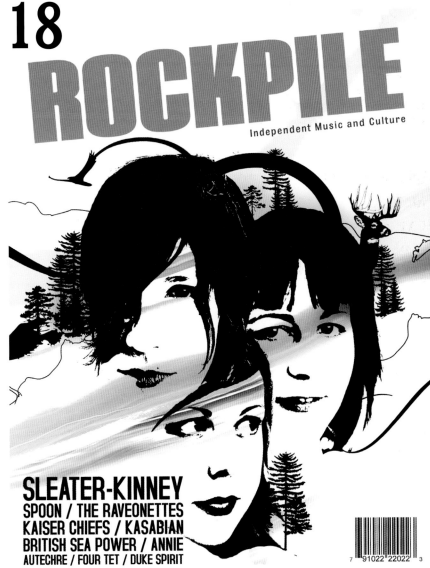

17. Ryu Itadani, *Akarium* magazine, "Omotesando," editorial.
18. Todd Breland, *Rockpile* magazine, front cover.

winter on the *Coca-Cola* side of life

19

20

21

Brands such as Levi's, Coca-Cola, Nike, Adidas, and Diesel, all keen to promote themselves as the epitome of "cool," look to illustrators to offer them street cachet.

23

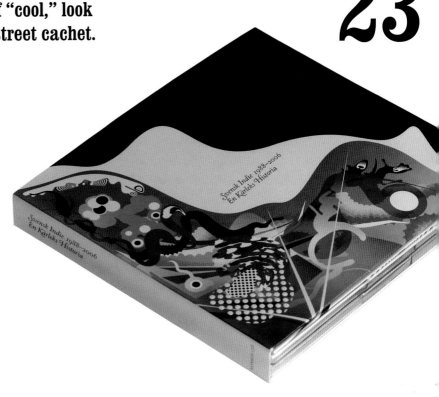

22

A future for fashion graphics

Much has changed in terms of the dynamics of evolution in fashion and music design. In a world where street culture and street style are snapped up and rethought—way before new movements can truly develop and find a new direction—to be returned to the consumer by huge corporations, new methods and approaches have emerged.

Brands such as Levi's, Coca-Cola, Nike, Adidas, and Diesel, all keen to promote themselves as the epitome of "cool," look to illustrators to offer them street cachet. It may be true that street culture died at the end of the twentieth century—more design comes straight from art schools than ever before—but finding innovative ways to promote fashion and music has fallen to a breed of designers and illustrators well-equipped for the road ahead.

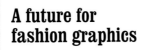

24

25

22. Christian Borau, *Trutx*, personal project.
23. Edvard Scott, North of No South Records, *Svensk Indie 1988–2006: En Kärleks Historia*, album cover.
24. Todd Breland, Elefant: *Lolita* single cover.
25. Marine, *Amelia's Magazine*, "The Trees," editorial.

27 **28** **29**

26. Maxwell Paternoster, Lines T-shirt design, personal project.
27. Barry Falls, *Gram Parsons*, personal project.
28. Uncompressed, *Hungaria Terras*, promotional poster.
29. Uncompressed, Hot Depot, music venue poster.

1

2

KE·ANE
UNDER
THE
IRON
SE·A

3

"My childhood summers in Finland inspired me," recalls Sanna Annukka. "I'd be out drawing most days, filling up sketchbooks. I remember reading illustrated books on folklore and fairytales and thinking I would love to illustrate such books myself one day."

KE·ANE
ATLANTIC

However, it wasn't children's book illustrations that brought Annukka's work to a global audience, but her first major commission—to create the sleeve artwork for Keane's all-important second album *Under the Iron Sea*.

"I was given a lot of scope to interpret Keane's lyrics and create imagery inspired by them," explains Annukka. "I didn't have to follow any strict criteria." The brief allowed Annukka to follow her ideal working method. "My work is all about the things I love; my passions, my fondest memories." The Keane artworks represent her interest in storytelling and narrative. She invented a strange underworld that unfolds beneath a wave of horses, each element created for the

album inspired by a different song lyric. "My real strength as an illustrator lies in creating a style that comes from the heart," Annukka explains. "I have spent years trying to work out what I want my work to reflect, and do justice to my passions."

Annukka's working methods developed from dedicating time to her drawing and sketchbooks, then translating her visuals in the print studio. This can be a frustrating process at times she admits. "My weakness is painstakingly redrawing images until I'm happy with them."

1.   Island Records, Keane: *Under the Iron Sea*,
     album foldout.
2.   Island Records, Keane: *Under the Iron Sea*, album cover.
3.   Island Records, Keane: *Atlantic*, vinyl box set packaging.

4

5

Nordic influences are self-evident in her work, but she'll never allow them to dominate. Scattered across the large wooden table in the living room of her home are some of her iconic reference books: 1950s and 1960s *Graphis* annuals and vintage children's books. They vie for space alongside her laptop, Wacom tablet, and lightbox. Annukka is planning to move her work from her home into a studio. "I'm setting up my own screen-printing studio," she explains. "It'll allow me to get out of the house more often!"

Despite creating every image for the Keane project on screen, it is Annukka's love of print that motivates her new work. Having set up her own company, she is now in the process of launching a range of limited-edition prints, looking to expand her range from fine-art prints to printed wall hangings, wallpaper, and screen-printed books. "I'm a printmaker at heart. I want people to be able to enjoy a print of mine in their home."

Is it only the fact that printmaking, unlike much digital illustration, creates a lasting physical form? "It is that, but also it is because it is so satisfying being so much more hands-on with my artwork. Screen printing is so involved and allows for much more experimentation. I also love the vibrancy of the colors you can achieve."

Annukka is excited about her new print works and is still developing ideas. "I have flurries of creativity. I constantly have ideas I'm grateful for. They all get written down, but not always instantly visualized," she admits. "There are days when I feel that I'm incapable of drawing anything good." Looking at her work it's hard to suspend disbelief, then quick as a flash she adds, " … and then there are days when I continue drawing into the early hours."

6

7

8

4. Island Records, Keane: *City In The Clouds*, album cover.
5. Island Records, Keane: *Octocity*, album cover.
6. Island Records, Keane: *Three Soldiers*, album cover.
7. Island Records, Keane: *A Bad Dream*, album cover.
8. Island Records, Keane: *Crystal Ball*, album cover.
9. Island Records, Keane: limited-edition lyrics book.

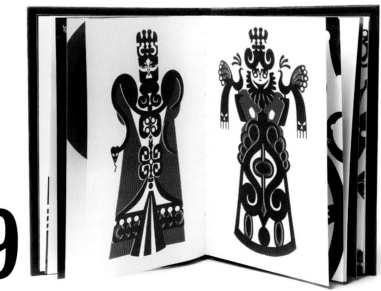

9

Profile: Sasha Barr

1

"I started freelancing purely for the fun of it," admits Sasha Barr from his home/office/studio in Memphis, Tennessee. "I had no intention of following it as a career, but as time went by, and the work kept coming, it began to take a priority in my life."

With no formal training as an illustrator or graphic designer, Barr completed undergraduate school in the spring of 2006 gaining a degree in Fine Arts from the University of Memphis. He specialized in printmaking. Barr's introduction to poster art occurred a few years earlier when, at the age of 19, in December 2001, he designed and printed his first poster for a local band.

Now continually striving to move his art forward, Barr's approach has a strong work ethic behind it. "I'm really just trying to keep working and exploring new avenues," he explains. "Over the past couple of years I've really focused on creating illustrative, yet graphic imagery, with a strong emphasis on typography and working all of the elements together." Barr's work is predominately music-related—the result of a conscious decision to work only in areas that interest

him. "I really enjoy creating my own visual interpretation of what other artists are doing in their genres, whether it's music or ideas or any other creative pursuit."

Unlike many artists who claim to be constantly working on ideas and visuals in a trusty sketchbook, Barr admits to using this method rather infrequently. "When I travel I'll use a sketchbook, but when I'm home, rarely. I'm just not a huge sketcher. I'll have a couple of different ideas swimming around my head when I start work on a project, and I just dig in. If a client requests multiple sketches or ideas for a particular project, then I'll do some roughs," he explains, not wholly disguising his disregard for this method of working.

2

3

1. Ann Arbor, *Broken Social Scene*, music poster.
2. *Philadelphia* magazine, "Chain Restaurants," editorial.
3. The Format: *Time Bomb*, single cover.
4. Kayo Dot, promotional poster.
5. The New Tragedies & Cory Branan, promotional poster.
6. Hothouse Flowers, promotional poster.

4

5

6

$4.99 US $7.60 CAN *Summer 2006*

7

8

LUCERO NORTH MISSISSIPPI ALLSTARS
CORY BRANAN DREW HOLCOMB

Without sketchbooks, layout sheets, roughs, or visuals to lead the direction of his work, Barr's formation of ideas isn't a labored process. "Of course, some projects can be harder work at the ideas stage—if I'm working on a band I'm not familiar with. Barr doesn't see this as a problem though. "I have ways of getting my brain working," he says with a smile. "I remember when I was at school, my writing professor always referred to the 'power of the white' when writing a paper, meaning that the most difficult bit is getting started. I really feel this is true of all of my commercial work."

Which leads nicely to the balance of commercial and self-authored projects in Barr's working week. Despite his fine-arts background he responds with a resounding, "Nowadays I spend nearly all my time on commercial projects, but for the future I want to expand my horizons."

7. *Skyscraper* magazine, *Skyscraper*, front cover.
8. North Mississippi Allstars, promotional poster.

Profile: Serge Seidlitz

1

2

1. *Chew Me A Flavor*, personal project.
2. *Little Orange* magazine, "Mixed Characters," editorial.

Describing himself as an "English/German hybrid born in Kenya who spent his childhood traveling between Europe and Asia," Serge Seidlitz understands his was anything but an ordinary start in life.

With a diet of *MAD* magazine and MTV fueling his desire to embark upon a career in illustration, Seidlitz undertook a design degree in London before taking his first job as an in-house designer at Cartoon Network. With four years of employment under his belt, he left the security of full-time employment for a freelance lifestyle. Never an easy choice, for Seidlitz it was the right decision: he was immediately approached to work on a range of high-profile projects, and the commissions keep coming.

Asked which of his recent back-catalog projects he is most proud of, Seidlitz reels of an impressive list: "the Vodaphone Airports campaign, the MTV Emerging Markets channel rebrand, the Match.com print

Seidlitz is keen to ensure that his clients are drawn from a range of areas within the creative industries. "If that's music and fashion, that's cool with me. Illustration and image-making coexist with them."

3. Vodaphone, World Map, ad.
4. Nelly Duff, *Heaven Sent and Hell Bent*, limited-edition print.
5. *Computer Arts* magazine, "Charity," editorial.
6. London Arts Council, London Map.
7. *GolfPunk* magazine, "Tiger Woods," editorial.

campaign, and the web and print applications for the Honda/Love Driving campaign," he coolly states. There are certainly equally impressive projects he could list from his portfolio of self-initiated work. When does he find the time to create projects outside the commercial arena? "Whenever I have time between commercial work." Either Seidlitz possesses brilliant time-management skills, or he is turning down the odd project from time-to-time.

"I try to make my work reflect my personality," he claims, "and I keep a part of me in all jobs, even if they're commercial. Color plays an important part, as does humor and detail. I like to keep people looking and seeing new things in my work." The detail in Seidlitz's images ensures the viewer's interest; the quality and intriguing nature of his drawings is paramount to their success. Seidlitz's work shows a unique touch, yet spans a range of associated styles. "My best ideas occur as part of a natural process. Once I have a rough idea of what I want to do, I just start and see how it evolves."

Seidlitz is influenced by music, fashion, his surroundings, and books. "I'm really into a book about Russian prison tattoos at the moment," he states. Not surprisingly, he is keen to ensure that his clients are drawn from a range of areas within the creative industries. "If that's music and fashion, that's

cool with me. Illustration and image-making coexist with them. As for influences from my surroundings, I share a studio near where I live. It's quite comfy. We have a video projector and a sofa to host film nights. We try to make it a nice place to hang out in as well as work in. It's also a bit of a bike-repair shop at the moment though. I have to admit there are a lot of Frankensteined eBay bikes hanging from the walls," he says, with the sound of resignation in his voice.

4

3

5

6

7

Case Study: Interactive Design

1

Music has always been the driving force behind Paul Farrington's outfit Studio Tonne, from creating digital, interactive sound-and-image screen toys to recording, releasing, and performing his own works, built using software he designed himself.

"It's all about music, or at least it always was …" explains Paul Farrington, the man behind Studio Tonne. He is attempting an explanation of his introduction to design when his mind wanders off. "Now much of the work is about the web, or at least it has been …" It seems that Studio Tonne's output is about to take another twist.

Farrington talks freely about new directions, but doesn't speak much about his work—he is keen for that to speak for itself. And speak it does, much of it in a digital sonic language. Farrington's prolific output has concentrated on the mix of sound and music with the visual, through the use of emerging technology. He began by creating sound toys—screen-based interactive visual and sonic treats—while a student.

Brian Eno described Farrington's output as "the new music," and *Wire* magazine named him an "interactive software visionary." Acclaim in the US followed with Disquiet describing Sound Toys as "one of the finest audio games on the web… deceptively elegant." Farrington's work turned heads.

Designing software to allow for the spontaneous generation of digital music gave him a platform for creating his own brand of music, which he then performed at various digital arts and music festivals across Europe. Studio Tonne went on to release CDs created using the software.

1. Studio Tonne, personal project.
2. Klitekture Records, website design and album cover, promotion.
3. Mute Records, *Noise Toy: Sound Toy*, promotion.

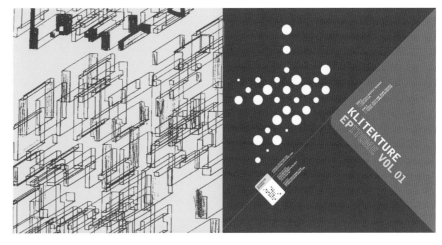

2

3

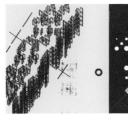

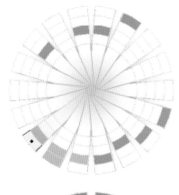
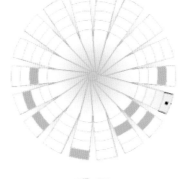
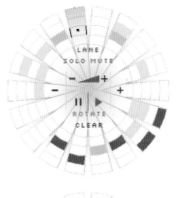

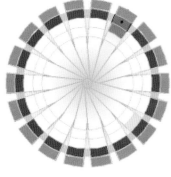
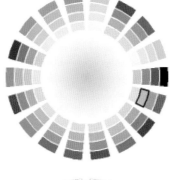
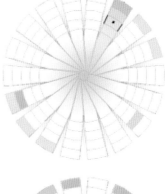

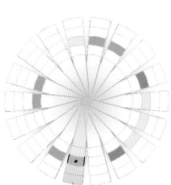
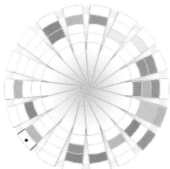
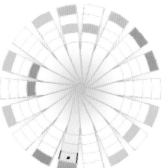

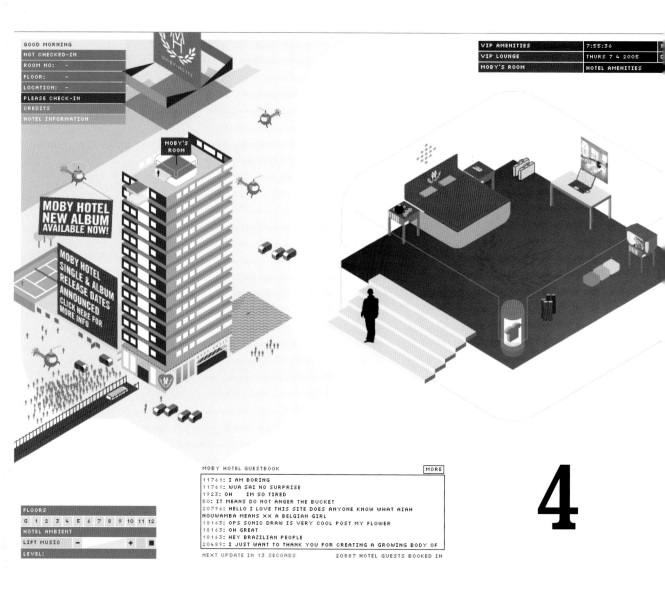

GOOD MORNING
NOT CHECKED-IN
ROOM NO: -
FLOOR: -
LOCATION: -
PLEASE CHECK-IN
CREDITS
HOTEL INFORMATION

VIP AMENITIES   7:55:36
VIP LOUNGE   THURS 7 4 2005
MOBY'S ROOM   HOTEL AMENITIES

MOBY'S ROOM

MOBY HOTEL NEW ALBUM AVAILABLE NOW!

MOBY HOTEL SINGLE & ALBUM RELEASE DATES ANNOUNCED CLICK HERE FOR MORE INFO

MOBY HOTEL GUESTBOOK   MORE
11761: I AM BORING
11761: WUA SAI NO SURPRISE
1923: OH   IM SO TIRED
50: IT MEANS DO NOT ANGER THE BUCKET
20796: HELLO I LOVE THIS SITE DOES ANYONE KNOW WHAT AIAH
NOUWAMBA MEANS XX A BELGIAN GIRL
18163: OPS SONIC DRAW IS VERY COOL POST MY FLOWER
18163: OH GREAT
18163: HEY BRAZILIAN PEOPLE
20489: I JUST WANT TO THANK YOU FOR CREATING A GROWING BODY OF
NEXT UPDATE IN 13 SECONDS   20887 HOTEL GUESTS BOOKED IN

FLOORS
G 1 2 3 4 5 6 7 8 9 10 11 12
HOTEL AMBIENT
LIFT MUSIC   -   +   ■
LEVEL:

4

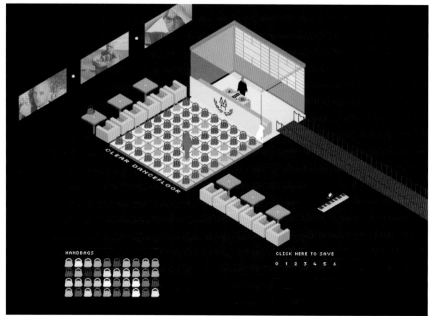

CLEAR DANCEFLOOR

HANDBAGS   CLICK HERE TO SAVE
0 1 2 3 4 5 6

Much, but not all, of Studio Tonne's early output was music-related. Clients were certainly keen to tap into his audiovisual digital aesthetic. These clients included Mute Records and Island Records, and soon non-music projects followed—for Katherine Hamnett, Prada, and Channel 4.

However, music design has remained central to Farrington's interests and continues to contribute to Studio Tonne's ever-increasing archive. As well as working closely with Mute on projects for Depeche Mode, Farrington has also designed a fully interactive website to coincide with the release of Moby's album *Hotel*. He created a virtual hotel for the site. Visitors "check in," are given a room number, and allowed access to facilities that include a disco with VIP area, and a tennis court where you can challenge Moby himself. The project displays much of Farrington's wit.

5

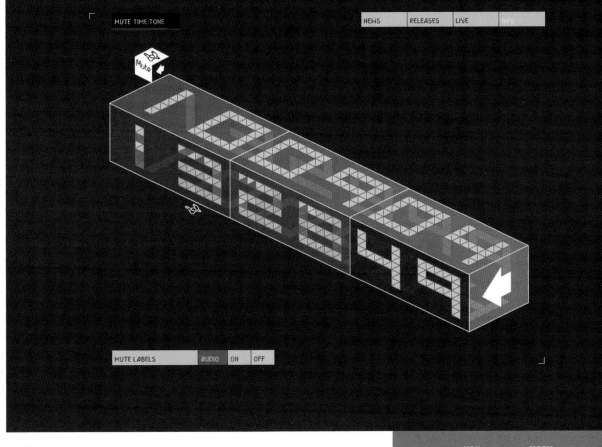

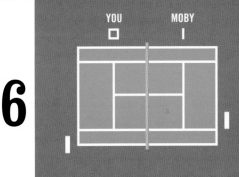

4. Moby, website design.
5. Mute Records, *Time:Tone* screen saver, promotion.
6. Moby, interactive game, promotion.

6

"It's all about music, or at least it always was ..." explains Paul Farrington, the man behind Studio Tonne. "Now much of the work is about the web, or at least it has been ..."

Keen to continue exploring new paths and ventures, Farrington starts to talk with much enthusiasm about a new direction in his work. "It's the first truly three-dimensional project I've been involved in," he says of a current project, still in production. "It's an interior—a 196m glass and recycled plastic walkway at Imperial College in London." Motivated to work on less transient projects than websites, which he describes as "like flyers," he has started to look for new challenges for Studio Tonne. "I'm really interested in making stuff, and working on things that will last a little longer." Farrington's description of his own design process is beautifully self-deprecating.

And just how did Farrington navigate his studio into pole position for a commission such as this, with no background in this aspect of 3-D design? "I don't know," he admits. "I think I'm just good with people." Not necessarily a given for someone who has spent the best part of the past decade staring at screens and listening to digital music.

Tutorial 5: Marine

Combining both photographic and drawn elements, Marine's creations are usually rich in color. For this image, however, to fit with the theme of a special issue of *DEdiCate*, she worked solely in black and white.

A commission for *DEdiCate*, the French lifestyle, arts, fashion, music, design, and movie magazine, gave Marine the opportunity to create this image of Ninja Tune's artist Simon Green, aka Bonobo. Her image was reproduced to run alongside an interview with Bonobo, a piece aimed to coincide with the release of his third album, *Days to Come*. For this special issue, *DEdiCate* had chosen the theme black and white, and all images, illustrative and photographic, had to follow this brief.

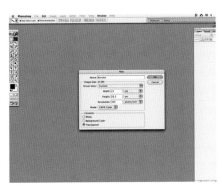

1 Marine's first step is to start with the blank sheet of paper, or in this case the blank Photoshop document, on her computer screen. Knowing that the final image was to be reproduced at 230 × 285mm (c. 9 × 11in), she opened a brand new Photoshop document, primed and ready for action.

2 The stock image provided by the magazine's art director wasn't ideal. The image lacked any real creativity. It was Marine's job to turn this around and make it look fun, fashionable, and funky.

3 Working with the Lasso Tool, she carefully selected each element of the image she wanted to use: the guitar, the amp, and Bonobo himself, of course. Gone for good was the less-than-attractive background.

4 On her Mac, in Photoshop, Marine clicked on Apple C and then Apple D to single out each of the three elements and past them onto a transparent background layer.

5 Her next step was to flatten the image, basically condensing all layers into one single layer, and convert the file from color into grayscale.

6 To take the image a stage further, Marine converted it into a bitmap at 300dpi with a halftone screen. This gave it the appearance of newspaper print, with its enlarged dots. Marine was now ready to apply her own take on the halftone process.

7 She then worked on "polishing" the visual effect. "I played with the frequency, angle, and shape to create the effect that I wanted here. I chose a frequency of 30 at 45°, with a Line shape."

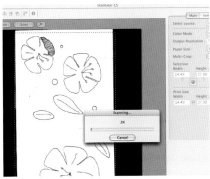

8 Away from the computer Marine created additional elements, some hand-drawn, some traced, and scanned them all in Photoshop at 300dpi.

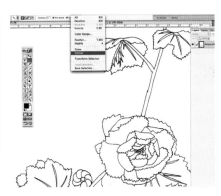

9 Still in Photoshop, she selected all the white space around these elements with the Magic Wand Tool, in order to add them to the final image.

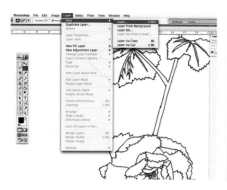
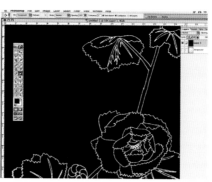

10 Marine then created a new layer in preparation for the next stage of the operation. While not a lengthy process in itself, this does require a little patience and practice.

11 Using the Paint Bucket, she filled this new layer with black and colored the white space. This gave the flowers a slightly imperfect appearance—just what she was after. She then turned off the layer holding the original scanned flower.

12 To remove the background black space, leaving just the black-filled flower, Marine carefully selected the outside edges of the flower with the cursor. Using the eraser function she then removed the black background.

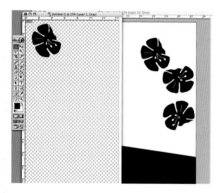
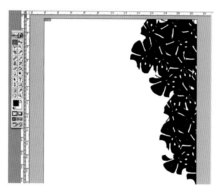

13 Following the same technique, Marine next selected a flower pattern she created previously as a hand-drawn and scanned element, and dragged this onto the final artwork canvas.

14 She then duplicated the layers, and rotated and shifted the elements to create the organic, floral patterns of the new background.

15 She treated her outline of Bonobo in the same way before dragging it onto the canvas. The final image was now starting to take shape.

16 The next stage of the process was for Marine to copy and repeat the silhouette of Bonobo, this time in white, and to add a black strip to act as a seat for him.

17 With this done, she converted the bitmap image back into grayscale, and dragged the layer she had been working on back onto the final artwork canvas.

18 Finally, she added the hand-drawn, scanned, and altered elements one by one, moving them carefully into place until she was happy with the overall arrangement. Her finishing touch was to add a strip of white stripes to create a cool black-and-white image with far more impact than the original ever had.

1

2

4

5

1. *Tricolore*, personal project.
2. *Yeah Yeah Yeahs*, personal project.
3. *Amelia's Magazine*, "The Pippettes," editorial.
4. *Muteen* magazine, "Horoscope," editorial.
5. *Amelia's Magazine*, "The Trees," editorial.

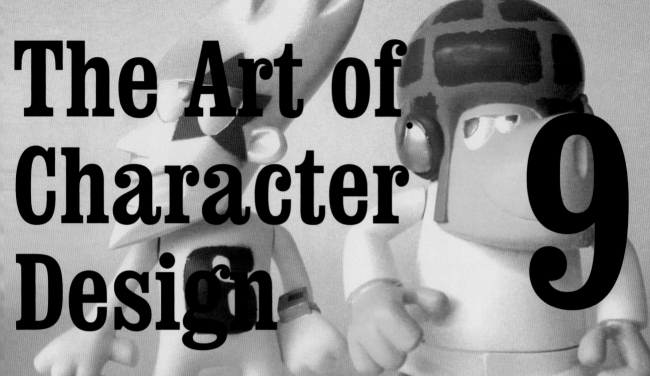

The Art of Character Design

9

Character design has been around at least as long as graphic design itself. The fascinating challenge for today's designers and illustrators is how to move the genre forward.

BEST DAYS
OF YER LIFE?

fortwo

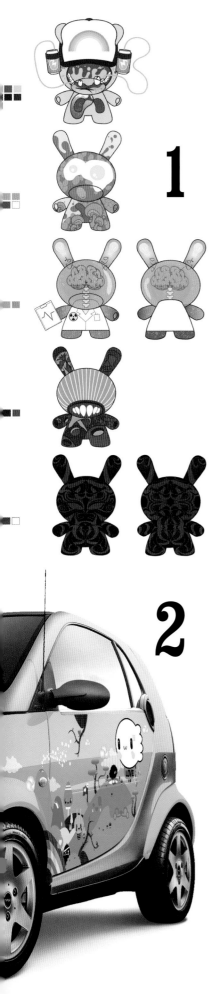

Global characters

Open your refrigerator, wander supermarket aisles, walk into any cool design studio, channel-hop, or plug into your PSP, and what do you see? From the Jolly Green Giant to Kaws, from Tony the Tiger to Sonic the Hedgehog, it's clear that the world of graphic design utilizes character designs in effective, proactive, and increasingly creative ways. The art of character design is alive and well and living in … well, just about anywhere that platforms, markets, and opportunities continue to open up.

History lesson

Where exactly did it all begin? This is impossible to answer, but the finger points at our cave-dwelling ancestors. In their quest to comprehend their place in the world, these distant relatives attempted to capture the essence and spirit of, for example, an animal that was to be hunted for food. They did this by painting directly onto cave walls, carving representational figures and animals from wood, or chipping them out of stone. Quite simply, these drawings and sculptures were man's first character designs.

1

From Tony the Tiger to Sonic the Hedgehog, the world of graphic design continues to utilize character designs in effective, proactive, and increasingly creative ways.

2

3

3 COLOUR MONSTER

1. McFaul, Kidrobot, designs for *Dunny* 3in series, vinyl figures.
2. TADO, DaimlerChrysler Smart Car, car graphics.
3. Andy Smith, Peskimo, 3 *Colour Monster*, Monster Mash trading card.

New technology

While technology has come on in leaps and bounds, and carving characters from wood or stone has since been replaced, in 3-D terms, by rotocast vinyl, the spirit of character creation remains the same. The joy, as a designer, in seeing your own character start to take shape, take on its own identity, begin to breathe, and then to walk by itself, can be compared with giving birth, though without the physical pain and the endless nappies. Sleepless nights, however, can often be part of the creative process.

Character design, despite its early beginnings, is a relatively new discipline, blooming at the start of the twentieth century. In their quest for greater revenue, many companies began to utilize the marketing power of personifying their products. Without the aid of huge advertising agencies, brand development teams, focus groups, art buyers, and account handlers, they began to promote their company's characteristics by producing their own company characters.

Old rubber ribs and the Jolly Green Giant

In 1895, the Michelin Tyre and Rubber Company introduced Bibendum, the Michelin Man, as their corporate character. Inspired by a stack of car tires "old rubber ribs," as he was fondly called, remains an iconic symbol to this day. Another who has proudly stood the test of time, albeit with a makeover or two, is the Jolly Green Giant. Launched in 1924, with a sense of style and a touch of friendly humor, the Green Giant symbolized the Minnesota Valley Canning Company. In 1999, celebrating his 75th anniversary, the Green Giant expressed this humor through a promotional campaign encouraging families to "Give Peas a Chance."

4

4.   Will Ainley, *Teenage Rock Monster*, personal project.
5.   Christian Montenegro, Levi's Argentina, Muertitos, ad.
6.   Junichi Tsuneoka, Moody Buddha, *Subway*, modular lampshade design.

5

6

7

M-I-C-K-E-Y

While static posters and trademarks captured the attention of the public, animated characters captivated their imagination. *Steamboat Willie*, released on November 18, 1928, marked Walt Disney's introduction of Mickey Mouse. *Steamboat Willie*, the very first animated short movie with a completely postproduced soundtrack of music, dialogue, and sound effects, set Mickey Mouse en route to global fame and fortune. After the Stars and Stripes, it is claimed that Mickey Mouse is the most recognizable symbol of the US. Ex-President Jimmy Carter even said "Mickey Mouse is the symbol of goodwill, surpassing all languages and cultures." The legal team for Walt Disney Productions expressed it well when they stated, "Mickey Mouse and his various friends are performers and salesmen who serve without pay. They work at all hours, whenever called upon. They are not temperamental and they need no union card. They need no food, no transportation, no lodging. But one thing is certain—they do need a lawyer!"

8

9

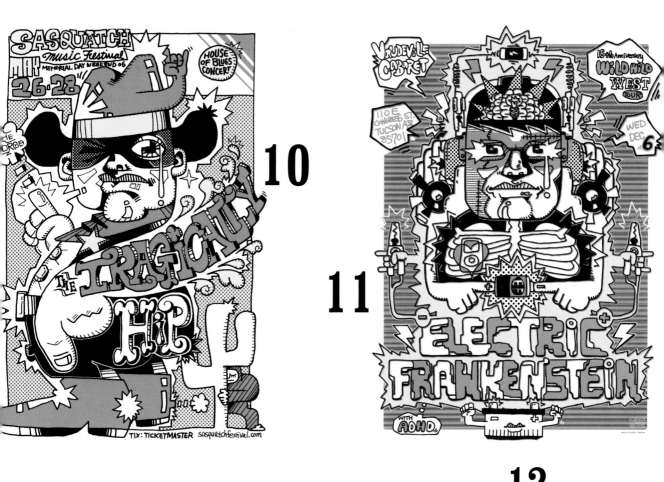

10

11

12

NOW WHERE DID
I PUT COLIN?

The battle of the video games

With the advent of the digital age, increased avenues for characters to parade along opened up, and it was the video-games' industry that paved the way. Inspired by a pizza with a missing slice, Namco designer Tohru Iwatani came up with *Pac-Man*'s look during a dinner with friends. Fifteen months later, with eight people working constantly on the software and another eight on the hardware, *Pac-Man* was good to go. In 1980, the year the game launched, 100,000 *Pac-Man* machines were made and sold around the world, making it easily, and still, the best-selling coin-operated game in history.

In 1982 another arcade game, *Donkey Kong*, appeared for the first time and became an instant hit. Shigeru Miyamoto, a Japanese games developer working at Nintendo, had created two characters that were to become iconic central mascots for Nintendo when introduced to gamers through *Donkey Kong*. It is hard to imagine a focus group today getting to grips with two overweight, badly dressed plumbers with ridiculous moustaches and oversized red hats, let alone giving them the green light. But the Mario brothers, Mario and Luigi, took the world by storm.

At the height of their popularity, a 1991 poll found that more children could identify a picture of Mario than Mickey Mouse.

Nintendo's vice-like grip over the gaming industry was to be put to the test. Rivals SEGA recognized that, alongside hardware and software developments, they needed to develop a company mascot to rival Mario. Yuji Naka and Naoto Ohshima, two artists at SEGA, were put in charge of the project and charged with the daunting task of wrestling gamers away from Nintendo with an icon that was instantly likable. And so, Sonic was born. The ultra-fast, spiky backed, finger-waving blue hedgehog with attitude was unleashed to rival Mario for cult status.

7.   Andy Rementer, Fresh Cotton, *Little Guys* fashion print.
8.   Nick Sheehy, *TV Monster*, personal project.
9.   Richard Stow, *Best Days of Yer Life*, personal project.
10. Junichi Tsuneoka, House of Blues, *Tragically Hip*, poster.
11. Junichi Tsuneoka, Electric Frankenstein, *Electric Frankenstein*, poster.
12. Richard Stow, *Now Where Did I Put Colin?*, personal project.

The designer toy

With gaming such big business, beating even Hollywood in terms of revenue, digital lifestyles appeared to be very much the way forward for character-based entertainment. And then something new bucked the trend. The desire for toys, designer toys at that, grew out of an emerging trend from Hong Kong and Japan. Collectible figures had been around for a while: Tintin, Astro Boy, Asterix, and many others were already changing hands for considerable sums. What was happening in Japan, alongside the growth of 3-D figures replicated from popular manga comics, was the creation of characters with no previous existence in cultural life; they had not appeared in a video game, comic, animation, or movie. The designer toy genre had arrived.

While youth culture, hip-hop, skate fashions, and street art merged; Keith Haring took to the New York subways with his own brand of poster art; and Futura 2000 customized box-fresh Nikes, a new interest in creating plastic toys and figures was germinating. A growing, but seemingly never-aging army of punters had started lining up around the block to get the first toy figures as they hit the stores.

In his book *Vinyl Will Kill!*, Jeremy of Jeremyville, in Sydney, claims the cultural phenomenon of designer toys began when Hong Kong–based artist Michael Lau took his customized G.I. Joe figures to a local toy show. He had reworked them "into urban hip-hop characters, wearing cool streetwear labels and accessories." Initially known as "urban vinyl," the accepted term soon became "designer toys."

As artists joined the global network of people interested in creating "cool" products, the market for these toys expanded. Kubrick, CRITTERBOX, Kidrobot, and other such companies sprang up to design, create, produce, and market designer toys aimed predominately at consumers living the designer lifestyle, creatives with ultra-cool, urban live–workspaces.

13

14

15

With gaming such big business, beating even Hollywood in terms of revenue, digital lifestyles appeared to be the way forward in terms of character-based entertainment.

From BMX bikes to KIA cars

16

Pete Fowler was in it from the start. Fowler grew up in Cardiff, Wales, in the 1980s, had ridden for a BMX team, skateboarded, and was heavily into music. At the end of the decade he left Cardiff to study fine art in Cornwall. He emerged, quietly at first, to be catapulted into the limelight with his work for Welsh band Super Furry Animals. Fowler picks up the story. "I was interested in sculpture, and to a certain extent toys, since I was at art school. I'd drawn several characters that I thought of as 3-D objects and started to sculpt them. I got a studio and made six or so large sculptures. I showed these at an exhibition in Japan and Sony Creative Products offered me the opportunity to design a range of toy figures. That's where it all started for me."

From this right-place, right-time, right-work starting point, Fowler launched his own website, Monsterism, and then his own company, Playbeast. Fowler describes Playbeast as "a small independent company with big ideas." It handles the manufacturing, marketing, and distribution of his creative toy output. So far, nearly 40 figures have been designed, manufactured, and made available for purchase.

For Fowler, "quite often the characters will come to life directly from sketches, regardless of the toys. I draw and redraw the characters until I'm happy with them, and they're suitable for sculpting. I like to make something new each time, and I try to communicate a parallel fantasy world that my creatures exist in," he says. "I like to engage people's imagination in the characters and the stories surrounding them. I do think that people's imagination is being deadened by worthless rubbish on TV," he states.

Despite Fowler's views on television programming, it is on your TV set that you can view his most high-profile commercial work to date: a range of characters created for KIA's four animated commercials. Fowler worked with Passion Pictures, using both CGI 3-D and stop-motion animation techniques, to create the ads.

13. Ian Stevenson, Pictoplasma, *Get Out!*, personal project.

14. Pete Fowler, Monsterism, Cam-Guin, vinyl figure.

15. McFaul, Kidrobot, designs for Dunny 3in series, vinyl figures.

16. Will Ainley, *Faesthetic* magazine, "Luvin' it and Eatin' it," editorial.

17. Pete Fowler, Monsterism, *Molvox Tribe*, vinyl figures.

17

18

19

Every product has a character

Commercial projects have kept TADO busy too. Designing a special edition Smart Car for DaimlerChrysler in Taiwan was an excellent departure for the duo. Characters adorn the model, but sadly it may never see the light of day outside Asia. "It would be amazing if stuff got to the next level here as it has in Asia where every product, it seems, has a character," they say.

Still, TADO remain busy with projects including mascots for British Airways, branding for MTV International, and numerous character/toy projects including their own toy line for Flying Cat, called Fortune Pork. The line currently stands at 13 unique figures, with Ryoko and the Sissyfits (a band with five members), in development at the time of writing. "We do think that the future is very exciting for smaller companies and freelancers who are now able to apply their distinct styles and approaches to bigger commercial projects," they say.

London to Paris via Hong Kong and Tokyo

Colette, the Paris-based lifestyle gallery cum shop with the motto "styledesignartfood," showcased London-based illustrator JAKe's break into 3-D character design, for adFunture. "That figure [an ape] was part of a show at Colette. They saw the prototype version and asked me to create a special edition in their own colors," he explains.

"Every character that has been made into a 3-D form," and that includes projects such as the JAKe Ape and BADjUjU toys, "has started life as an image which has evolved out of my sketchbook; a character that I, or in some cases other people, keep coming back to," JAKe says. "Many have been used elsewhere, for instance on T-shirts, which means they are recognizable by the time they become a 3-D product," he adds. JAKe continues to work with adFunture, based in Hong Kong and Shanghai, and Comme des Garçons in Tokyo. When asked where he sees his craft heading, he is quick to quip "onwards and upwards, or charity shops and bargain bins!"

18. TADO, Playlounge, *Fortune Pork* series, key-chain toys.
19. JAKe, Jake Toys, *BADjUjU*, vinyl figures.
20. TADO, Taipei Toy Festival, *Puchoo*, vinyl figures.
21. JAKe, Jake Toys, *Enough Apes Already*, vinyl figure.

Character design remains an intrinsic aspect of modern graphic design. It is hard to ignore, but harder still to quantify the impact it has had on commerce and entertainment.

The future

Character design remains an intrinsic aspect of modern graphic design. It is hard to ignore, but harder still to quantify the impact it has had on commerce and entertainment. Gazing into a crystal ball might reveal what the future holds, but this group of global artists has its own opinions. "I'd like to see a greater use of the ornamental combined with the functional," admits Pete Fowler. Jeremy offers a warning. "The designer toy genre needs to diversify, spread out, and always keep fresh. It needs to reinvent itself with new directions based on art and ideas, and not just commerce." It would appear that the future of character design rests with artists and their sketchbooks.

22. Nick Sheehy, *Bulbship*, personal project.
23. Christian Montenegro, *Zutana*, personal project.

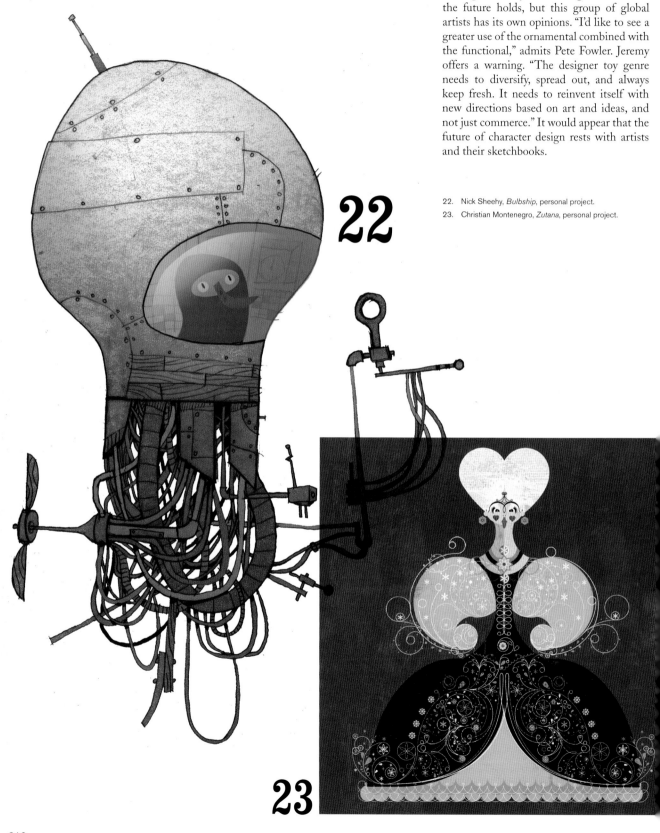

22

23

1

2

"Check e-mails, think about heading down to studio, make elaborate lunch, upload photo of lunch to Flickr, check e-mails, chase up payments, head down to studio, doodle, paint, mess about, leave studio, check e-mails, start thinking about dinner, sleep, wondering where the day has gone." Jon Burgerman describes his average day.

Burgerman has made a name for himself. His "doodles," as he refers to them, are known across the planet. Creating sticker sets, limited-run books, and commissioned art on hotel walls, along with animations and campaigns for major brands and companies, Burgerman has certainly been a busy guy.

And all within such a short time! Burgerman graduated in 2001, with a degree in fine art rather than design or illustration. US artist Jean-Michel Basquiat proved to be an influence on his work. "He really had the biggest influence on me, from an early age," he recalls. "Seeing his work made something click inside my head and my hand."

1. *Zeebzeebs*, personal project with Flying Cat, plush toy.

2. Candy Culture, *We heart Candy*, ad.

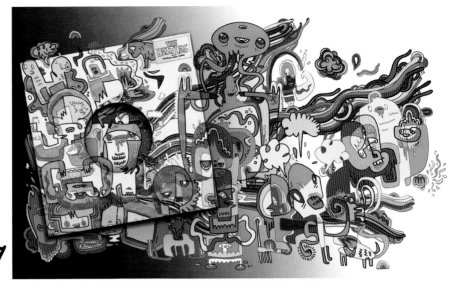

7

Burgerman's world still reflects something of that early influence. "The work I create generally occupies a screwed-up, hyper-emotional, drawn world inhabited by mischievous and ambiguous characters. If it's about anything, in a general sense, it's about an overwhelming anxiety pushing my mind into a confused, yet colorful state." Burgerman's reflections on his work and the demands it places on him suggest a twisted therapy. It might be that he needs the work more than it needs him. "I am anxious, often have a feeling of disconnection, and have a real need to retreat into fantastical skewed realms," he utters with a sense of the dramatic, yet with a genuine, heartfelt reality driving the claim.

Burgerman works at a frenetic pace, partly to meet demand from clients, but also to fulfill his own ambition to get work into as many places as possible. Recent projects have seen him create a monster 27m (88$\frac{1}{2}$ft) timeline for "Game On," an exhibition at London's Science Museum. The piece featured a snake-like monster that depicted illustrations of cultural and video-gaming icons set into the different "time bellies" of the character. Even Burgerman admits, "it was a lot of hard work!" Commissioned to "doodle" an entire hotel suite in just two days, from floor to ceiling, without any preplanning, Burgerman reports that his only problem was "'some minor hand cramps!"

Busy he might be, but Burgerman isn't convinced that he works hard at what he does. "My weaknesses include being lazy, stubborn, reluctant to travel, not great at web stuff. I have a low patience threshold for animation work, and I'm easily distracted and don't have a great knowledge of design history. Oh, the list goes on!" Perhaps he is a perfectionist? "No. All of my characters have something wrong with them—imperfections add character," he chuckles.

3. Mimoco, Mimobot, art toy USB memory stick.
4. Yummy Industries, *Burgerland*, fashion wear.
5. Nineteen Seventy Three, box, ad.
6. Character stickers, personal project.
7. *Creator Studio Magazine*, "Tomorrow Never Knows," editorial.
8. *Burgermenos*, personal project with Flying Cat, vinyl toys.

Profile: Simon Oxley

1

2

"My SoHo is a 13 × 13ft room with a homemade desk on shaky legs. I work on a Mac G5 Quad, 30in Apple monitor, and shoot images using a Canon EOS 5D. Sometimes I release stress by banging the hell out of a set of drums in the room," explains Simon Oxley on a tour of his studio.

More specifically, Oxley and his alter ego idokungfoo inhabit Fukuoka, a town on the southernmost Japanese island of Kyushu. A country town steeped in a rich heritage, it was the landing point for the Mongol invasion, eventually crushed by the Kamikaze or Divine Wind. The studio's backdrop is a series of mountains, quite different from Oxley's first setting in Japan. "I worked for three years for a multimedia company in Harajuku, in central Tokyo. I was thrown in at the deep end in terms of culture shock, but I soon realized that the culture here isn't so shocking, it's just different enough to inspire new ideas for my design and illustration," he reasons.

Now a permanent resident in Japan and married with two young children, Oxley recognizes the influence that the cartoons he watches with his kids has had on the development of characters in his illustrations. "I've found this to be a great source of inspiration. It motivates me to concentrate on the ideas behind stylistic considerations."

Oxley has been quick on the draw when it comes to utilizing technology and the Internet. "I've been uploading images to iStockphoto.com in recent years," he explains. This slightly undersells his relationship with the company—his present catalog of images stands at over 2,500, he was responsible for designing the company identity, and he

1. *Magic Makers*, personal project.
2. *Break Time at the Lab*, personal project.
3. *Tasty Wildlife*, personal project.
4. *Sweet Tea T-shirt design*, personal project.
5. Postcard set, personal project.

3

yummy...

4

card design by simon oxley idokungfoo.com

5

works on their ad campaigns alongside many other forms of promotion and merchandise. "I really feel that the images I've been uploading recently display my current visual thinking. It has provided me with the motivation to make drawings on a daily basis like never before in my career," he says.

Other recent developments at idokungfoo include the launch of a merchandise brand featuring the characters Oxley has been developing in recent years. His cute, but left-thinking folk are now appearing on greetings cards, postcards, posters, and T-shirts, and the range promises to continue expanding. It is clear that Oxley's equal blend of humor and cuteness have struck a chord, and he has plenty of work to keep him occupied.

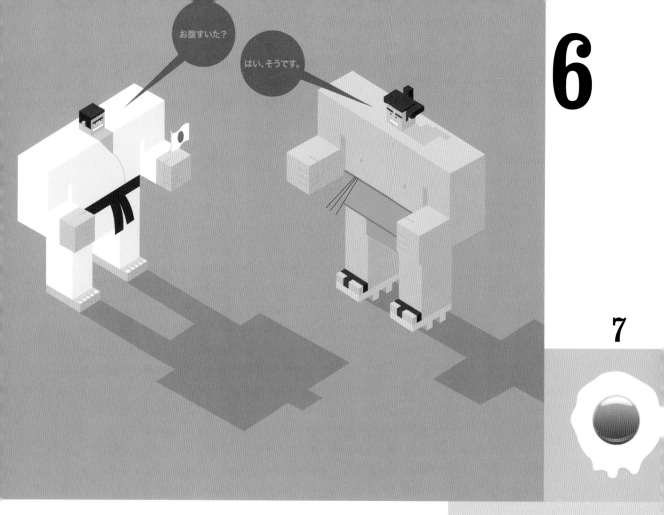

"I worked for three years for a multimedia company in Harajuku, in central Tokyo. I was thrown in at the deep end in terms of culture shock, but I soon realized that the culture here isn't so shocking, it's just different enough to inspire new ideas for my design and illustration."

However, he wants to keep his work in perspective, so he makes time to relax and enjoy family life. "I spend much of my free time nurturing the children with plenty of play in the open air, and letter and number learning," he explains. Time separate from his fix of watching cartoons with them.

Oxley calls an end to his working day to meet with his father-in-law. "We practice golf at the driving range together. He's just finished life as a salary man in a career that allowed him to hit many golf balls, so he's the perfect coach for my amateur swing. I think he's hoping that I'll improve to the point that our 18-hole games might involve a little more competition for him." Perhaps Oxley should get his father-in-law up to speed on the idokungfoo drum kit.

6. *Hungry Again*, personal project.
7. *Good Morning*, personal project.
8. *Once Upon a Time*, personal project.

"Coming up with ideas is not the problem, the true art (and business) is actually choosing the order in which to do the stuff so it vaguely resembles a proper career and not just creative ramblings. "

1

Jeremyville

2

3

Jeremyville is up and at it early. "I'm up at 6.30am, take a run along the Sydney Harbour foreshore, then it's a 5-minute walk into the studio for an 8.30am start," he states in a matter-of-fact way that plays down his lifestyle. Living in a Potts Point apartment and working in a four-story Darlinghurst townhouse (terrace) has its benefits. "I see a row of terraces bathed in bright Sydney sunshine out of my studio window," is his description of the neighborhood. "Darlinghurst is a cosmopolitan, creative suburb with Italian cafés serving great coffee, as well as art stores, clothing boutiques, and chic apartments." It's a tough environment for creativity!

Jeremyville kick-started his career while still at university. He began by cartooning for the *Sydney Morning Herald*. While this is not unusual in itself, he wasn't studying graphic arts, but majoring in architecture.

1. Toy 2R, *Sketchel Kid*, designer toy.
2. Jeremyville painting a 60in (150cm) *Qee*.
3. Toy 2R, *Bunny Qee* "Petting Zoo," designer toy.

5

6

4

subway worm
eating the big apple

"I appreciate and strive for the uncluttered, distilled form, and lack of ornamentation and decoration in my character designs. I try to refine them to their essence and only include the details necessary for conveying the message. I've learned when to stop drawing."

"I had no real desire to practice as an architect: that would have involved working for another studio before setting up my own. I just didn't want to wait that long to start creating." Not afraid of stepping forward, Jeremyville approached the *Herald*. "It's Australia's leading daily newspaper. My first job was there, at the age of 19," he explains. "I never really 'worked my way up.' I just went in with some drawings from the student newspaper I edited and got a job straightaway. By the time I graduated, my art career was already in full swing, with various freelance commissions, so I just moved into that full-time. I started to employ assistants at the age of 22."

Despite turning his back on life as an architect, he remains influenced by the modernist sensibilities of Le Corbusier and Alvar Alto. "I appreciate and strive for the uncluttered, distilled form, and lack of ornamentation and decoration in my character designs. I try to refine them to their essence and only include the details necessary for conveying the message. I've learned when to stop drawing," he states. Jeremyville sees his mission in character design as "the constant refinement of the idea and reduction of the linework, to arrive at something sublime and effortless, yet loaded with atmosphere and imagery."

Despite wanting his work to look effortless, in reality his projects require a huge amount of effort. "I always feel that I'm just starting. There are always new projects, new books … lots of sketchbooks of ideas waiting to become real."

4. Trexi, Trexi Series 3 packaging.
5. Trexi, 10in Trexi "NYC," designer toy.
6. Strangeco, Self Portrait as Circus Punk, designer toy.
7. Toy mashup, self-promotion.

7

Tutorial 6: Jeremyville

Jeremyville's characters have always played a big part in his studio's creative output, whether in a sketchbook, applied to a print project, or, as in this case, as a commissioned 3-D toy.

Creating toys is no simple affair. It can take anything from 3 to 12 months of designing, refining, modeling, and prototyping to realize a character and manufacture the finished toy. Jeremyville was approached by Red Magic in Hong Kong, as part of its Love Original toy project, to create a character with a unique take on the whole genre. Following time spent negotiating both the design brief and the contract, via e-mails between Sydney (home to Jeremyville HQ) and Hong Kong, he was ready to begin the project.

1 Each and every Jeremyville project starts in the same place—his sketchbook. Always to hand, the book is home to doodles, sketches, and drawings that can help kick-start any design. "Drawn in cafés, in the studio, anywhere and everywhere, the aim is to create interesting silhouettes and starting points."

2 As refinements are made, a distinct look for the character begins to emerge and slowly take shape. The drawings are worked on, in pencil and marker, until a final black-and-white version is reached.

3 Once a final character is decided upon, Jeremyville scanned the sketch into Photoshop and colored the figure digitally. The chosen character for this commmission was loosely based on a self-portrait, complete with sketchbook in hand. The concept—25 Hours in Jeremyville—was then e-mailed to the client.

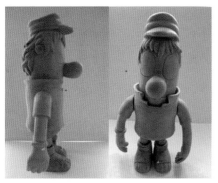

4 The next step was for Red Magic to commission a sculptor to model a 3-D version of the character, drawn directly from the original sketches. At this stage Jeremyville was e-mailed digital photos of the model to check for accuracy.

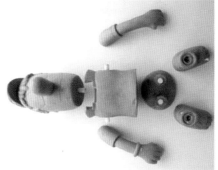

5 Each individual part of the toy was shot for Jeremyville to check: it was important that every component be considered at this stage, and vital that every aspect of the detail within the drawing was translated into the 3-D model.

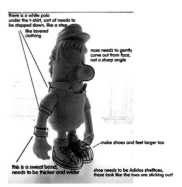

6 Jeremyville marked any changes required on a low-res file and e-mailed this back for the sculptor to take in the changes. This was a crucial stage in the development of the project as changes of this nature cannot be made at a later date.

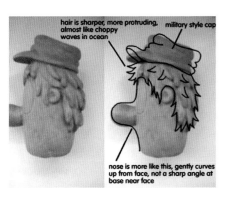

7 Basic changes, such as proportion and scale, hair, and nose were all detailed. At this point the team decided to remove the hat as it was not working well enough visually.

8 Next, a more detailed "turnaround" was created. This Photoshop file, an image of the toy from front and back, showed the sculptor all the nuance and detail that would be visible in the final design.

9 At this stage the sculptor sent 3-D models for Jeremyville's approval, and some minor modifications were agreed.

10 The next stage in the process involved the creation of black sculpts, or wax molds, and Jeremyville confirmed that the hand intended to hold the sketchbook was set to the correct angle and width. Because it becomes much harder to make any changes at this stage, any further changes are likely to impede the project schedule and increase costs.

11 Having decided that the toy is likely to be much more popular than initially envisaged, Red Magic asked Jeremyville to work up some color variants. He designed three more and sent these to Hong Kong.

12 With the character in production, it was time to start developing the custom-designed packaging. Jeremyville turned to his sketchbooks for inspiration once more.

13 Once the design was complete, a mock-up of the pack was created so that, just like the model itself, the product could be checked from every angle. While it was only output onto simple lightweight stock at this stage, this allowed a judgment as to how successful the design was.

Red Magic ©

14 Red Magic e-mailed Jeremyville its logo to add to the packaging graphics. Branding is important to the project's success: many toys will sell to people interested in Jeremyville's work, and it will also appeal to collectors of everything that Red Magic produces.

15 A 24-page full-color booklet was designed for inclusion in the pack to act as a promotional device for the toy. As part of the deal, discussed with Red Magic before the project got underway, Jeremyville negotiated run-ons for his own use too.

16 To start promoting the toy, Jeremyville designed a series of mash-ups—collages made from elements of the toys and packaging—for use on his own website. "It is a good idea to slowly introduce a project," he states.

17 There was much anticipation waiting for the final pieces to arrive in the studio—would the figures look and feel as intended—and great joy in seeing the very accomplished final toy. The translation from 2-D sketch to 3-D toy took time, but was well worth the effort and the wait.

18 With the toy completed, Jeremyville turned his attention to another, related product—the Sketchel. This bag is decorated with a special 25 Hours in Jeremyville graphic. Purchased through the Jeremyville website, the Sketchel adds another layer to the entire project.

1

2

1. Toy 2R, turnarounds for *Bunny Qee* "Petting Zoo," designer toy.
2. Trexi, color palette for *Trexi* "Ghost of Andy," designer toy.

Commercial Art and Personal Projects

All illustrators agree that maintaining a body of noncommercial, self-authored work keeps things fresh, informs commercial projects, and leads to new opportunities.

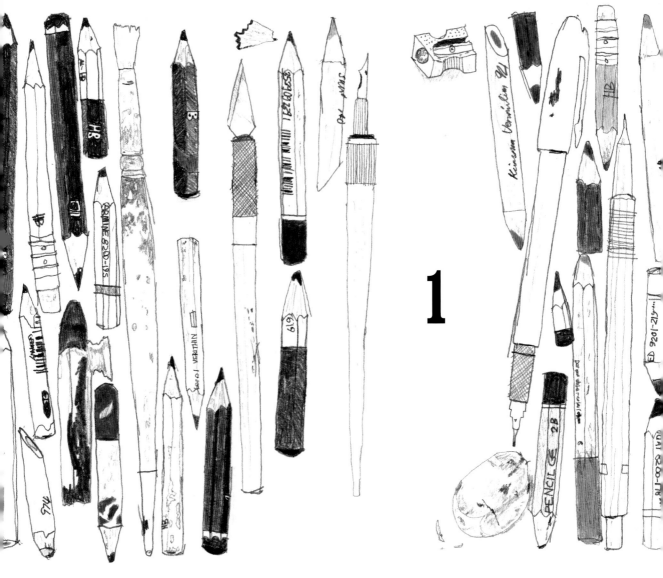

Finding time

"It can be really difficult finding the time for personal projects in between commercial commissions and earning a living," admits David Sparshott, an illustrator new to the scene with only 18 months of freelance work under his belt. "It is often during the times when I'm not looking to do any personal work that I'm suddenly inspired by a random encounter," he continues. "It is those moments, however, that keep me motivated and interested in further developing my own work."

Keeping things fresh, finding inspiration for commercial projects and investing them with new ideas and new working methods, as well as creating the space and the time to invest in personal, self-initiated projects is never easy. It is crucial, however, to maintain a healthy balance of work and play in order to move one's work on conceptually and stylistically. Neil McFarland, who chooses to both exhibit his work and undertake commercial commissions, has his own philosophy and approach when it comes to carving out chunks of time. "I work when I'm paid to and undertake my own work after hours and between projects. However, when I get a special idea, I do turn down commercial projects and stick to my own work until it is all done." McFarland, having worked as an illustrator for nearly a decade, has fine-tuned his working strategy to great effect. "It is very rewarding," he continues, "becoming your own boss. You're the best person in the world to work for. Note the word person," he adds. And this is where the McFarland philosophy really kicks in. "In this industry, you are your own brand so it pays to keep this in mind and make sure that you have some kudos," he says.

1.   David Sparshott, *Pencils*, personal project.
2.   Ian Stevenson, *Rubbish*, personal project.

3

Building your own brand

McFarland's brand, Paris Hair, enables him to be viewed as more than just a jobbing illustrator; it allows him the freedom to undertake cartooning and animation, and to exhibit his work as an artist. "The only way is to have some principles and stick to them," he exclaims. "Keep doing things that you enjoy, keep making images that we all want to see. Everyone working in illustration should be an inspiration to everyone else in illustration."

Karin Hagen, Swedish born and working out of Stockholm, is already starting to build her own brand despite having been practicing for less than two years. Hagen's website is deliberately low-key and low-tech. It combines a unique and playful typographic sensibility with her illustration work.

With an approach that combines the surreal with the naive, and a style best described as honest, her images are witty yet somehow echo the innate sadness in her subjects. "I'm trying to make my personal projects commercial," she admits. "I've been drawing my whole life, but I only recently started to do it professionally. I've still got my day job though."

It is unlikely that Hagen will have time for that day job for much longer. With things really starting to fall into place—she has work included in a book alongside 14 other illustrators, all funding its publication though they live and work in very different parts of the globe—Hagen's work is about to be seen by a much wider audience. Not one to rest on her laurels, she has also completed her first range of jewelry. "I'm very proud of it," she admits, then adds a charming reflection of her work as a designer and artist. "Creating gives meaning to my life."

"The only way is to have some principles and stick to them," McFarland exclaims. "Keep doing things that you enjoy, keep making images that we all want to see. Everyone working in illustration should be an inspiration to everyone else in illustration."

4

Commercial concerns

Increasingly, illustrators are moving into the creation of a range of products; they are becoming less interested in treading the traditional routes of illustration and more inspired to initiate projects that hold a special interest for them. Whether it offers commercial potential or not, illustrators are starting to bend the rules. No longer content to sit and wait for the phone to ring or an e-mail to arrive, illustrators are taking control over, and responsibility for their next move.

Of course, illustrators have always put on exhibitions—they offer a fantastic way of meeting clients, raising a profile, selling work, and making some money—but this new approach seems very different. Illustrators on the fringe appear to be hosting group shows, creating catalogs, holding openings and private views for their peers rather than their clients. Pure, unadulterated commercialism isn't where it's at; the movement is much more about creating work that feels right and looks good than acting as a promotional vehicle for a portfolio of glossy finished work.

3.   Adam Hayes, *Consanguineous*, personal project.

4.   Tim Hill, *Bricobrack*, personal project.

5.   Karin Hagen, *The World Does Not Care About Me*, personal project.

6.   Chris Dent, *Brooklyn Bridge*, personal project.

Chris Dent, an illustrator who cites influences as broad as architecture and hip-hop, and who's work has been reproduced in *Lodown*, *Noise*, and *Dazed & Confused* magazines, recently mounted an exhibition of his large-scale drawings. Entitled "Hey Man Hatten," the work was a body of drawings based on famous New York City sites and landmarks. Created five years after 9/11—Dent stood on the viewing platform of the World Trade Center just a few weeks before the tragic event—the work has a very personal perspective.

As for the working processes that Dent employs … "I like to work directly onto the paper using pen rather than a pencil. The process allows me to be adventurous," he admits. "This is where I feel that my interest in street art is apparent too. Having that rawness of an immediate drawn line brings a freshness to my work."

The exhibition took over a month to orchestrate, allowing Dent time to take on just a couple of commercial projects at the same time. Dent works passionately on new projects and isn't one to grumble about a long working day. In answer to how he juggled the pressures? "I guess I just made the time by working around the clock. But from my point of view, at the moment, it's just a privilege to draw for a living."

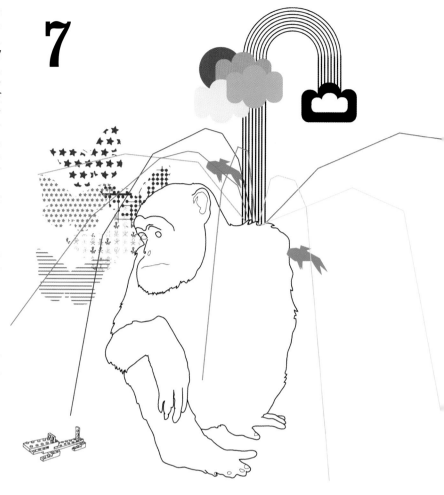

7. Kate Mockford, Rainbow Ceramics, *Aimless Ape*, promotion
8. C'est Moi Ce Soir, Magic Pony gallery, *He Lives*, promotion
9. Tim Hill, *Everbody Into the Place*, personal project.

Home meets gallery

Christopher Green and Gary Barber work under the name C'est Moi Ce Soir. They may only have been working together for around three years, but already their output has been quite considerable. Firstly, renovating and restoring a four-story Georgian property is quite an undertaking. The building, or more accurately the squat, which had been unused and unloved for many years, now acts as home and gallery for the two artists.

Complete with a sculpture garden, the home/gallery is already enjoying positive press, and the building's landlords have given permission for the artists to stay as long as they like. Exhibitions at the house have been well received—audiences and art critics have responded with genuine interest in the projects. C'est Moi Ce Soir works across many media and describes its activities as "painting, drawing and collaging, self-publishing books, designing bespoke items of clothing, and working with music and animation." With a client list that includes the *New York Times*, Somerset House, and *Amelia's magazine*, the duo have recognized that their approach to dividing time between commercial and personal work is paying off. "However, to be honest," admits Green, "much of our time these days is spent working on self-initiated artworks including books, animations, clothing, collages, and sculptures. That's where we get the most out of working as a duo."

From London to Tokyo

Ian Stevenson has created commissioned works for MTV, Pictoplasma, Mother, and E4, but is mostly interested in creating his own work. "I do as many self-authored projects as possible. I think of an idea and I do it." A recent book project, *Lost Heroes,* concentrated on "actors who never quite made it and what they are doing now." The book, a collection of 22 postcards, was printed in a limited run of 500 copies. Stevenson's simple graphic screen prints, based on real signage, but with his own quirky alterations, have become collectible, selling out online immediately.

Stevenson cites "everyday life and the everyday strangeness of people and the world" as his main influences. He has certainly found a niche market for his books and prints, adding T-shirts and sweatshirts to his growing list of products. It is, however, Stevenson's limited-edition take-out coffee cups, printed with a face exclaiming "Rubbish," that demonstrates just how far the potential for creating quirky products has come.

The fashion giant Paul Smith hosted the exhibition Happy London at his SPACE store in Tokyo. Billed as showcasing the works of young, new, and established artists and illustrators from London, it included four new Stevenson works. Stevenson takes up the story. "Each one of the six artists was handpicked by Paul Smith, as he felt that they embrace the positive spirit of London in 2007," explains Stevenson.

9

11

12

So, where next?

For some, it is clear that managing a mix of commercial and self-authored projects can be a really positive experience. Combining the pathways of exhibiting artworks, making and publishing one's own publications, and designing products, as well as creating work in response to a client brief can certainly pay dividends, both creatively and financially. Balancing the two is a matter of preference and, to some extent, self-control. To ensure that there are enough hours in the day, it is crucial to manage time effectively. Be realistic about meeting deadlines. It's important to have an understanding of just how deep your commitment must be to making a business work as that is exactly what working as an illustrator, designer, and increasingly as an artist, is about—running a business.

15

Combining the pathways of exhibiting artworks, making and publishing one's own publications, and designing products, as well as creating work in response to a client brief, can certainly pay dividends, creatively and financially.

Renewed optimism

There is a real sense of optimism in contemporary illustration, a feeling that the discipline hasn't just returned to form after its years in the wilderness during the 1990s, but has moved dramatically on. Applications to illustration courses at art schools and universities are up, more magazines and publications are dedicated to illustration than ever before, and galleries are exhibiting the work of contemporary illustrators in a way that has not been seen since the late 1970s. With big businesses harnessing the talents of illustrators to give their brands unique personalities, and ad agencies increasingly turning to illustrators when searching for "cool" ways to promote their client's products, it is clear that illustration has much to offer again.

Can the current boom in illustration continue? Will the bubble burst and the discipline retire back to the spare bedroom, exiting the cool studios of East London, the Lower East Side of Manhattan, and the former industrial warehouses of Berlin? What is different about illustration's popularity this time round is that, against the tide of conformity, against the sea of mediocrity, it is now all about individual voices and visual languages.

The digital collages that first appeared at the tail end of the 1980s, with the rise in popularity of the Mac; or the faceless, nameless, vector-drawn Illustrator and Freehand images of the 1990s have been replaced by a new raw, honest, and more diverse aesthetic. A renegade band of illustrators and image-makers has entered the discipline with a greater focus on experimentation. Taking risks in their work, they have a desire to push the traditional boundaries of contemporary illustration.

Some of the ground once occupied by designers and artists is being invaded by illustration. No longer content to wait for incoming commissions, illustrators have gone out in search of artistic and commercial opportunities. Filled with a new confidence, they will continue to shape the future of this ever-mutating discipline called illustration.

16

18

17

16. Gemma Correll, *Does Not Play Well With Others*, personal project.

17. Chris Dent, *Empire* magazine, "Don't Panic," editorial.

18. Adam Hayes, *RCA* magazine, cover.

Profile: Jim Stoten

1

"My current studio," explains Jim Stoten, **"is a temporary space in my girlfriend's mom's house."** He may have a temporary studio, but his commitment to illustration is anything but. **"I have never ever considered doing anything else. Ever."**

Jim Stoten is driven. He has to be. He draws every illustration, commissioned or self-initiated, by hand—no computer trickery for him, just good old-fashioned handcrafting. While the digital will play a part in the final delivery of his work, and he occasionally scans a drawn image to create a visual, or to place objects in order to make decisions about compositions, it is with the pencil that he makes his marks.

"My desk is home to a computer," admits Stoten, "but next to it I have a tin containing pens, knives, rubbers, and pencils. That's what I use."

2

1. *Boing* fanzine cover, personal project.
2. Medeski Martin and Wood, Gomez: *Catch Me Up*, single cover.
3. The *Guardian*, "A Snowman's Story," editorial.

"I awake," he states, "I look out of the window and recite some poetry to the gathering woodland creatures there. I saunter down the stairs and prepare myself a warming beverage."

3

4

5

Stoten's work, which includes an array of complex characters, has a surreal sense of the unreal. This doesn't just sit within his work—he has a left-field perspective on life in general. His description of a normal working day reveals his take on life as an illustrator. "I awake," he states, "I look out of the window and recite some poetry to the gathering woodland creatures there. I saunter down the stairs and prepare myself a warming beverage. I then shower, dress, and get on with work of some kind. Then I go to bed." If only life really were that simple.

A keen and active imagination is very much part of Stoten's life, and his working methods and approach to image-making have developed from a desire to enter a world of his own creation. Storytelling is another characteristic of Stoten's work, and his character development is beautifully demonstrated in his graphic novel *The Diamond,* of which he is justly proud. "My work is escapism, pure and simple," he states. What Stoten wishes to escape is unclear, but when asked where his ideas

come from he lists a few driving factors. "Sugar rushes, anxiety attacks, drifting off, listening to old records with odd chord structures, eating Skittles, and …" his mind wanders off again "… and dressing up," he adds without the subtlest hint of sarcasm. "I'm influenced by all sorts of stuff—Tove Jannsen, Edward Gorey, Tom Waits and Jim Jarmusch in *Down By Law,* French music … all sorts really."

Asked what he struggles with, Stoten is brutally frank and honest. "I think I could be better at the part where you talk to people for the first time." What does the future hold? "You're asking the wrong person because I just don't know," he remarks, as if he truly believes that someone else does hold the answers. "If I had to guess, I'd say crippling creative agony, melancholic rainy Wednesdays, and frantic scribbling coupled with highs, fulfillment, and joy. So long as I have plenty of commissions coming in, and plenty to do, I'll be a happy old illustrator," he admits, and, after a moment's thought adds, "with a beard."

4.   *The Diamond,* personal project.
5.   *Boing* fanzine cover, personal project.

Profile: Emily Alston

1

"I think that, as with most creative careers, it's not really a case of you choosing to pursue it, it chooses you, if that makes sense," explains Emily Alston. "All people working within the arts have a strong creative sensibility that lies within them. I guess the decision that you make is how you choose to express it."

2

Emily Alston is in her studio, best described as an expression of her creativity. "I suppose some people would describe it as a mess," she explains. "It is filled with pieces of ephemera I've collected that inspire me—old postcards, badges and beer mats, brown paper and envelopes, wallpaper samples … Some work by Eduardo Paolozzi and images by my favorite photographer Walker Evans are pinned on the wall, as well as some photocopied samples of work by designer Elsa Schaperelli, alongside examples of my own work." Alston uses her studio walls for her own work to "see if it stands the test of time." While she works, she listens to talk radio. "Often it's just as background noise. It can be very relaxing," she admits.

Emily Alston has only been working for a short time, following her graduation and time as an intern working for various design companies, but she is already well established as a designer and illustrator. She has worked with many leading companies, including Paul Smith, the *Telegraph*, the *Guardian*, and *Dazed & Confused*. What is it that appeals to these clients? "Nearly all of my work has a nostalgic feel to it," admits Alston. "This is

1. The *Guardian*, "Origami," editorial.
2. Orange, Balloons, ad.

4

5

3

because most of my references are from the past, despite the fact that I use computers to generate it. The work can often take on a screen-print aesthetic."

Alston is at ease when speaking about her work. She understands the direction she wants to take it in and where its appeal lies. "Visually, it is usually simple and bold—a combination of flat color and found paper textures." When asked to judge her own strengths she smiles and says, "I have a good sense of color and composition, and I can generate visual ideas pretty quickly, like most image-makers, I guess. I think in pictures."

Alston's work has a unique appeal and, despite surrounding herself with ephemera and the work of others, she has always focused on creating her own individual voice. "You can't help but be influenced in some ways by the work of other designers and illustrators," she admits, "but this doesn't mean that you should slavishly copy a certain style or a way of working." Despite being a relative newcomer to the industry, Alston

"I have a good sense of color and composition and I can generate visual ideas pretty quickly, like most image-makers I guess. I think in pictures."

demonstrates an understanding of how it works. "Illustration is particularly fickle," she continues. "Styles come in and out of fashion. That's why it's so important to develop your own way of working and your own ideas; it ensures you are separated from the hoards of people who are also making pictures."

The subject of Alston's pictures depends on the project. "Commissioned work can often be dictated by the client, but personal work usually involves things I'm interested in: animals, children, and oddities. I suppose that they are childish creations for adults," she reflects.

6

8

6. A Swarm of Angels, *Angels*, promotional poster.
7. The *Telegraph*, "Rabbits," editorial.
8. Emily Forgot, 2005 calendar, personal project.

Profile: Craig Atkinson

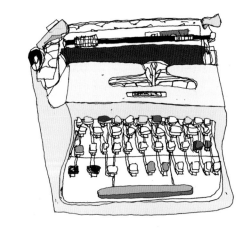

1

"I like listening in on conversations and making up stories about the people and what they must be like, where they live—that kind of thing. I probably get it all wrong though," admits Craig Atkinson.

2

Craig Atkinson is surrounded by packing boxes, awaiting a studio move from a room in the flat he shares with his wife to a much larger room in their first house. "I can't wait. I'll be able to make 10 times more mess and hopefully 10 times as much work. I've already got a huge desk and some green plastic chairs with wheels, and plan chests and stuff and …" It is evident that Atkinson really is excited about the move.

And he does need more space. Having switched from abstract artist to illustrator, he is now establishing his own web-based publishing house meets gallery meets online arts club. Café Royal has a wide-ranging mission. It features a shop selling artwork, zines, magazines, artists' books, prints, etc. Its first project, *Café Royal 1*, is a collaborative venture—a 175-page book featuring the work of 14 artists. Atkinson enjoys working with other artists, having curated exhibitions with many artists around the world.

POETS OF OUR TIME

3

Atkinson's move from fine art to illustration was prompted by his growing boredom with painting large abstracts. "I decided to go back to basics. I started to draw with a pen and pencil on paper, and from there decided to try to get work as an illustrator. It worked. I've recently been commissioned by the *New York Times*, Orange, and *Esquire* magazine, and I've had my work featured in *The Times*."

Keeping the balance between commercial and personal work is a battle that Atkinson has well under control. "If I'm not working on a commission then I'm working on my own stuff," he states. "I would never want to do commercial stuff 100% of the time, but I wouldn't want to do anything 100% of the time!" Currently, the balance falls in favor of self-initiated work. "I have lots of ongoing work in this area, with a number of books and exhibitions happening."

By way of explaining his often surreal subject matter and images Atkinson offers, "I think my work is about storytelling. I don't necessarily know what the story is, and the viewer wouldn't either. A lot of my work is suggestive of something. My abstract drawings and paintings look as though they should mean or represent something. Often the titles will suggest something way beyond what the image will suggest. The two things together can be amusing, banal, or just pretty weird," he laughs.

"I think my work is about storytelling," offers Atkinson by way of explaining his often surreal subject matter and images. "I don't necessarily know what the story is, and the viewer wouldn't either," he admits.

Atkinson also has a range of practical, hands-on considerations. "I think breaking things down to colors and shapes really helps with composition, although sometimes I just switch concerns like that off and do the first thing that comes to mind, then I work over it, and then again. Often the most successful pieces happen this way," he adds. "I kind of encourage mistakes and accidents and work with them."

5

6

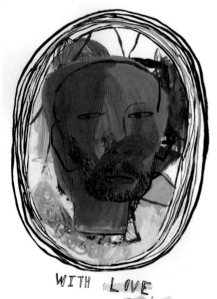

4

Social Club is Craig Atkinson's limited-edition, A5 book for Café Royal, his web-based magazine. Self-funded and self-published, its 150 pages are all drawing, no text.

Craig Atkinson, the founder of Café Royal, enjoys the creative freedom of self-publishing projects—no client restrictions, his own flexible deadlines, overall responsibility for the content, design, and marketing of his own products. It might sound simple; it can be anything but.

For Atkinson, self-publishing is simply a route to getting his own projects out into the world. With Café Royal acting as an online gallery and shop, Atkinson has also created the beginnings of a successful route to marketing self-published projects, including his book *Social Club*.

1 The concept for *Social Club* was simply to bring together a collection of back-catalog drawings from previous sketchbooks. "To make a book you need content," explains Atkinson. "In this case the content was some of my drawings, selected from finished pieces and from my sketchbooks."

2 Atkinson began by investigating other books. "With anything new, you should research what is already available. It's a great excuse for buying new books," Atkinson offers. "I wanted to look at print quality, covers, binding, dimensions, page layout, etc. I also like the feel of zines, so I had to buy some of them too!"

3 Having completed his research, Atkinson had to decide on what format his book should take. "I decided to keep *Social Club* fairly lo-fi. I wanted the book to have a similar feel to the sketchbooks the drawings came from."

4 Decisions about the final layout needed resolving before Atkinson could move on with the project. "I wanted images to run off the page, as they would in a sketchbook. I didn't want color print, other than on the cover. And I wanted the book to be A5, about the size of my sketchbooks, perfect bound, and a paperback," he details.

5 Atkinson next spent a few days looking at printers and binders. "I'd used a 'print on demand' website before. The results were OK, but this time I wanted to work with local printers, so I requested some print quotes. I chose a local, family-run firm," he explains.

6 The next stage was to make final decisions on the content. "I needed to narrow down the initial selection of 300 drawings to 150—the number of pages in my book. The 150 that didn't make it weren't necessarily worse, they just didn't sit as well with the rest of the work," admits Atkinson.

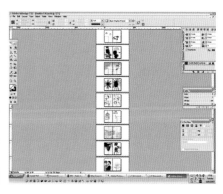

7 With the selection complete, he then scanned each of the sketchbook images, then corrected the scans for contrast and brightness before resizing them in Photoshop. Much of this was very simple, but time-consuming work: as each of the images had different qualities, they couldn't be batch processed.

8 To design and lay the book out, Atkinson used InDesign. As there was very little text, this was a relatively simple job. The hard part for him was deciding on the image order. "To start with, I just put an image on each page," he admits.

9 Having taken this approach, the pages then needed ordering. "I started to do this taking into account how the meaning of each image changed depending on the image before or after it. Low-level semiotics, I suppose," he suggested.

10 Next came the title. "*Social Club* came about through making lists of possible titles, basically because I like the sound of it. I also like the connotation of somewhere slightly dark, beat up, friendly, with sofas, TV, live music, cheap beer, etc. A social club is also somewhere that people get together—kind of what the drawings are doing."

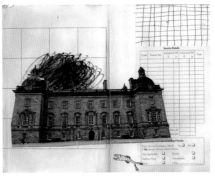

11 Atkinson next looked into the issue of obtaining an ISBN for the book, knowing it would help with cataloging and selling. He opted to buy the minimum allocation an individual can purchase in one batch—10.

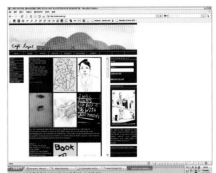

12 The benefits of an ISBN may not at first be obvious. "I set up Café Royal to work both as a publisher, and as a shop to sell the book, so the details on the ISBN are Author: Craig Atkinson, Publisher: Café Royal, and a few details about the book itself. Now any bookseller can key in my ISBN and all the details will appear, along with how to order the book," he adds.

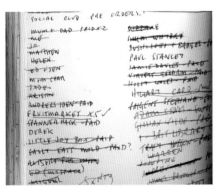

13 Marketing began early. "I started taking pre-orders about two months before I collected the book from the printers. This initial bit of marketing helps to spread the word that the book is on its way," advises Atkinson.

14 "One of the most exciting parts of the process is seeing the initial proof." Atkinson opted for digital proofs bound and finished rather than wet proofs straight from the press as that would give him a better idea of how the final publication would look. Wet proofs would give a clear indication of the print, but couldn't be bound until dry.

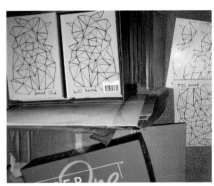

15 Atkinson then took delivery of the printed, bound, and finished books. "If all is good that's great; if not, this is your last chance to get anything done to improve it. Check each page and the construction carefully."

16 Atkinson sent 20 promotional copies out to companies and people he thought were in a position to review or promote the book in some way. "I normally send a couple of other things too, badges and stickers etc. Of course, family will want copies too," he explains.

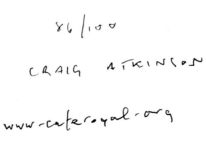

17 More useful advice from Atkinson. "Keep marketing and aiming to sell your books until you've nearly run out." As an incentive he offered the first few signed and numbered.

18 Atkinson was successful in selling his first edition and looked toward printing a second. "The printers should give you a discount this time, as plates don't need to be remade. If they don't, ask for one," he advises.

SUNDAY AT THE SAVILLE

1. *Sunday at the Saville*, personal project.
2. *Shed*, personal project.

Professional Practice

Insider Tips for Illustrators

Work smarter not harder, and keep your head above water with these insider tips, facts, opinions, and suggestions.

Some of today's hardest-working illustrators take time out to bring you their top, glistening, information-packed gems. Carefully mined from real-life experiences, these handpicked nuggets will help you advance your career.

Get the lowdown on starting up your own studio, promoting your work, the pros and cons of agents, getting a portfolio to work effectively, winning clients and new business, pricing jobs, inspiration and collaborations, and how to structure your working week in order to fit it all in.

Part 01: Getting to Work

TIP 01: AN EDUCATION IN ILLUSTRATION (1)

Be willing to learn through practice. Many illustrators swear by the education they received as full-time art students, while many others maintain that learning on the job is the best route. Steve Wilson notes, "I made loads of mistakes when starting out. There's a lot that can't be taught—you have to do it in practice."

TIP 02: AN EDUCATION IN ILLUSTRATION (2)

Look out for the pitfalls. Picking your own way through the minefield of contemporary illustration practice isn't easy. McFaul declares, "Although the education I received was second to none, I'm still under the impression that when we left education, we were dropped off in the middle of nowhere, blindfolded!"

TIP 03: THE DAILY "ROUTINE"

Create a daily structure that works for you. Life as an illustrator is never dull. It can be completely rewarding one day and just as frustrating the next. But being your own boss, while demanding, is an attractive lifestyle. JAKe, illustrator, cartoonist, and animator, explains, "I haven't had a 'real' job for 10 years. I'd find the structure too hard. One of the highs of life as an illustrator? There's nobody telling me what time to get out of bed!"

TIP 04: STUDIO SETUP (1) WHERE?

Make sure your own space suits your needs. Setting up a studio is a crucial first step. If funds for start-up costs and overheads are low, this first studio may well be where you live. Jody Barton, illustrator with Big Active, describes his space. "Two wobbly desks, two computers, and a telephone, in the middle of nowhere. From my window I can see a truck on the way to the slaughterhouse."

TIP 05: STUDIO SETUP (2) WHEN?

Wait until finances allow you to set up a studio, but do it before it starts to affect everyone you live with. You'll know when the time has come to set up your own studio away from where you live. It will either be space limitations that force the move; a partner demanding the spare bedroom back for visiting guests; or the kitchen table heaving under the weight of a Mac, monitor, scanner, printer, external drives, digital camera, and a mountain of art materials.

TIP 06: STUDIO SETUP (3) WHY?

Why work in illustration when it can appear such a haphazard career? Jon Burgerman, illustrator and king of doodles, admits, "it can be isolating, but it turns your hobby into a job." McFaul goes the extra yard with his advice for aspiring illustrators. "Think lifestyle, not job." Get involved in illustration because you love doing it, not because it appears a smart career move. As Jody Barton states, "Make work that is your own, not what you think will get you a big ad campaign!"

TIP 07: STUDIO SETUP (4) HOW?

Seek advice from those who have already set up a studio, ask questions of Internet service providers and telephone companies, view a number of spaces before you make a final decision about somewhere to rent. "My working environment," explains Michael Gillette, "is a small, cramped room, although I am moving to a new, larger studio. I've always worked in incredibly chaotic places. It doesn't seem to affect my work though."

TIP 08: TECHNOLOGY— LIFELONG LEARNING

Become friends with a technical whiz kid or learn how to keep your kit in tip-top condition yourself. Understanding software and hardware issues isn't a choice—it's a

"We are the music makers and we are the dreamers of dreams." Richard Ardagh

necessity. The pros of the digital era outweigh the cons, as far as Gillette is concerned. "The flexibility of illustration in the digital age is a huge bonus," he states. "It allowed me to move from the UK to the US after all."

TIP 09: LEGALITIES (1) THE TAXMAN AND THE ACCOUNTANT

Enlist the services of a good accountant— one who understands the creative industries. It pays to be legal, make no mistake. Ian Wright admits that his accountant has "bailed me out many times. He could be the key to my survival!" JAKe also advocates being organized from the outset, though he admits to being a little lax himself. "For me, it's receipts in a shoe box until I really have to look at it!"

TIP 10: LEGALITIES (2) THE SOFTWARE POLICE

Be street legal and avoid the temptation of using anything other than legitimate software. Designers and illustrators do get prosecuted—don't think it doesn't happen. Update regularly (most updates can be skipped every other version if you need to save funds), and keep abreast of new software developments by reading reviews and trying 30-day demos.

Part 02: Getting the Work

TIP 11: SELF-PROMOTION (1) ISSUES, IDEAS, STRATEGIES

Decide what works for you, but whatever methods you choose, avoid annoying the people you're marketing to. Some illustrators advocate simple procedures. Patrick Thomas of Studio laVista offers straightforward advice. "Do every job as well as you possibly can; that's the best way to promote yourself." Jon Burgerman agrees. "The best method of self-promotion is to do great work and get it seen."

TIP 12: SELF-PROMOTION (2) PORTFOLIO DO'S AND DON'TS

Prepare your portfolio well, keep it organized, and look after it. It is a valuable tool. Anthony Burrill, illustrator/designer, offers useful advice. "Keep it simple, with a good mix of self-initiated and actual commissions. Make it look professional. Use good-quality printouts on decent paper." Steve Wilson

suggests, "Put your hand in your pocket and invest in leather. Your book will be going to big ad agencies, competing against other illustrator's portfolios for the same job."

TIP 13: SELF-PROMOTION (3) ON-LINE PORTFOLIO DO'S AND DON'TS

Set up a web-based portfolio. These can be even more useful than a leather-bound portfolio for reaching a wider audience. Richard May, cofounder of Pixelsurgeon and Black Convoy, reckons "better 20 large images than 60 tiny ones," and advises, "Make sure the presentation does your work justice—keep it simple and to the point."

TIP 14: SELF-PROMOTION (4) ATTITUDE AND COMMITMENT

Hit the streets and see lots of potential clients with your work. Ian Wright advises, "Take notice of their reaction to your work and don't be afraid to ask for advice. We were all new to the profession once." Patrick Thomas offers clear-cut thinking. "Be prepared to work bloody hard if you are going to get anywhere." Anthony Burrill quotes from one of his own letterpressed self-promotional posters, "Work hard and be nice to people!"

1.   Richard Ardagh, greetings card, personal project.

TIP 15: DATA MANAGEMENT—KEEPING CONTACTS

Get a good database application or get used to using a digital address book, and spend time keeping it up-to-date. It will take up huge chunks of time later if you don't. Miles Donovan of Peepshow explains his own procedures. "All my contacts are on my Mac and iPod and are regularly updated and backed up. This is all-important!" Peepshow's work-experience people "phone around asking for names and emails of art directors, which is handy," he admits.

TIP 16: WINNING CLIENTS AND BUSINESS

Ensure that your work is visible, and being seen by the right people at the right companies—that is, those in a position to commission. There is no magic formula for getting the job, nor wand to wave to ensure success. It can be down to luck, but more often it is down to graft and persistence. Original work that is well executed and communicates clearly will find admirers.

TIP 17: PITCHING—DO'S AND DON'TS

There are occasions when a phone call from an art director puts you in an interesting position. As he/she explains, the agency are doing a pitch for a client and if it comes off there will be a lot of work for you, all very well paid. But, in order to win the pitch, they need you to work frantically for 48 hours and can only offer you a pittance. What do you do? Only you can decide. Perhaps it'll help you win the project; perhaps it'll be lots of work for no gain…

TIP 18: AGENTS—PROS AND CONS, UPS AND DOWNS

Think about getting an agent. There are so many arguments for and against agents, but the bottom line is that a good one can get you work you wouldn't have time to chase, or even know existed. "My agents in New York," explains McFaul, "are worth their weight in gold, but I'm also very proactive." Donovan agrees. "Agents find work you wouldn't normally get, command higher fees, and offer support if things go wrong."

TIP 19: AWARENESS OF INDUSTRY DEVELOPMENTS

Check sites such as Design Observer and Pixelsurgeon on a regular basis to ensure that you're always up-to-date. Being aware of what's happening in the design world is crucial; keeping abreast of recent projects by other illustrators through news and reviews in magazines will help too. These activities are a valuable means of research.

2. Christian Borau, Limited Editions/New Factory, promotional poster.

TIP 20: MEETINGS—HOW TO CONDUCT THE PERFECT BUSINESS MEETING

Arrive early, do your homework, be organized and well groomed. Know who you are seeing and something of the work the client has recently created. Large design and advertising agencies make this easy for you by having their press releases bound and on display in their reception areas. Take a notebook and pen to the meeting and ask questions if you are unsure.

Part 03: Doing the Work

TIP 21: WHAT MAKES A GREAT IDEA

A great idea will communicate your thinking and message without the need to talk it through. Remember, you'll not be there to explain your illustration to everyone who views it! Knowing how to recognize a strong idea takes time and experience, though being aware of when your creative thinking is not up-to-scratch is a good start.

TIP 22: IDEAS—HOW AND WHEN TO GET THEM

There's no surefire, tried-and-tested method to guarantee you a great idea, but the uncertainty and buzz you'll get from the pressure of having to come up with one is a powerful drive. JAKe reflects, "On a good day, it feels like they come out of nowhere. Just grab your sketchbook and pencil, start loosening up, and see what happens."

TIP 23: VISUALS—FROM BEER MAT TO MOOD BOARD

There is no rule of thumb to help here. Work out what is best for you. There are as many styles for illustrators' visuals as there are styles and ways of working. Experience will help you gauge how much work you need to undertake to get your idea across. Some art directors demand a high level of finish, others are happy to have a chat on the phone or via email to discuss ideas, and then let you go straight to artwork.

TIP 24: ORIGINALITY—WHY YOUR OWN APPROACH IS BEST

To survive in illustration, you need to offer a unique take on the world around you. Having your own visual language will get respect and work from commissioning art directors. "There are far too many illustrators and designers churned out of colleges," states Patrick Thomas. "You are competing in a very strange environment against a huge number of talented and determined people," adds Jody Barton. "Make your own work."

TIP 25: WORKING PROCESS—MAKING LIFE A LITTLE EASIER

Have a game plan, understand where you are right now, and where you would like to be in a year. Plan carefully, structure your week and your month, decide when to make appointments with potential clients, and when to update your website. Michael Gillette recalls advice given to him by another illustrator. "What have you done today to show the world that you exist?"

TIP 26: PRICING (1)
DO'S AND DON'TS

Firstly, don't panic. Secondly, take some time out. If you are offered a fee over the phone, ask for five minutes to have a think and offer to call back. Use your five minutes wisely. Compare the job with your previous experience, and check previous commissions to gauge if the fee seems fair. Speak to another illustrator if you need a second opinion. If asked to name a price, put the boot on the other foot—ask what the budget is. Every job has a budget!

TIP 27: PRICING (2)
WHEN TO WORK FOR NOTHING

Nothing upsets illustrators more than discussion about free work. Michael Gillette believes illustrators should "only work free for charities. It devalues the whole industry if you work for nothing, so don't do it." Patrick Thomas, guided by his principles, states, "A job that has no production budget is simply not worth doing. But I don't regard making an antiwar piece, for example, as a 'job;' I consider it a moral obligation."

TIP 28: PRICING (3)
COMMANDING THE BEST FEES

Advice about commanding top dollar for your work varies. Jody Barton believes it is wise to keep in mind exactly what you do. "You are a professional, mostly with a qualification, and sooner or later you'll have bills to pay." Never ever charge less than you can afford to live on: most of the work you do should demand somewhat higher fees.

TIP 29: DEADLINES AND STICKING TO THEM

Late nights working against the clock, working throughout the week and through the weekend into the following week ... illustration rarely allows a nine-to-five life. There are simply some projects that demand high levels of input to meet the deadline. Your professionalism is not only judged by your output, but also by your ability to deliver on time. "To miss a press deadline is inconceivable," stresses Patrick Thomas.

TIP 30: HOW TO DELIVER THE GOODS

If you want to work for a client a second time, make sure that their experience of working with you is a positive one. Being available on the end of a phone, answering emails within a reasonable length of time, and communicating regularly with your client all helps ensure that you come across as a professional.

Part 04: Working it Out

TIP 31: RESEARCH AND DEVELOPMENT—NEW APPROACHES

It pays dividends to reflect upon your working methods and processes occasionally. Illustration isn't an exact science; illustrators all have their own approach to making images and their own creative journey. McFaul describes his. "Draw, paint, cut, scribble, splash, scan, photograph, coffee, phone calls, email, draw, paint, manipulate, stare out of window, laugh, fiddle, scan, manipulate, go out, come back, scan ..."

TIP 32: INSPIRATIONS (1)
LOOKING AND LEARNING

Keep a constant lookout for inspiration. Creative meanderings or visual wanderings can add untold pleasures to an illustrator's archives and collections. Inspiration can come from anywhere—a color combination spotted and photographed for later perusal; a torn, discarded scrap of paper with just part of a smudged image, but with a unique visual language ...

TIP 33: INSPIRATIONS (2)
A LIFE OUTSIDE ILLUSTRATION

Don't spend all of your time submerged in illustration: it isn't healthy to live within just one discipline. Of course, illustration takes dedication and long working hours, but you need to emerge once in a while and live the rest of your life. Michael Gillette keeps his head out of illustration to find references and inspiration. "I like old nineteenth-century stuff at the moment. It's better to be inspired by an esoteric reference than a contemporary one."

TIP 34: INSPIRATIONS (3)
PAST GLORIES

As illustrators we dream of creating iconic works. Enjoy the dream! For most people—illustrators and civilians—key illustrations define moments in their lives. Album and CD covers, posters, or book jackets, whatever the work, images are significant.

TIP 35: NEW AVENUES FOR YOUR WORK

Explore new avenues for your work. Never satisfied, illustrators are constantly on the prowl for the next fix. Getting a job is a great high, doing the job another head rush, but illustrators constantly strive to get their work into new fields. Ambitious illustrators yearn for an array of canvases. Austin Cowdall at NEW, and a Black Convoy member, wants it all, "... more collaborations, more live illustration, painting, exhibitions, publishing, and chaos!"

TIP 36: COLLABORATIONS (1)
WHO, WHERE, AND WHY?

Work with other people. Working with other like-minded, or unlike-minded, individuals opens up possibilities and new connections. "Sometimes it's all peaches and cream, sometimes it's chalk and cheese, but it's all good," explains Austin Cowdall. McFaul, a cofounder of Black Convoy, has his own take. "It's an educational experience that can open up many avenues. You can benefit from the opinions of others." Neasden Control Centre (NCC) agree. "It's healthy and keeps you fresh."

TIP 37: COLLABORATIONS (2)
RISK AS A LEARNING PROCESS

Step into the unknown—creatively, this can be an excellent pick-me-up. Ensuring that the repetitive process of commission, creation, delivery, and invoicing is injected with moments of madness is an important way of remaining open to new ideas. Jon Burgerman explains a recent project. "I'm working with a Danish artist, Sune Ehlers, on Hello Duudle books. I've never actually met or even spoken to Sune, but the process of bouncing JPEGs back and forth over email yields new ideas."

TIP 38: PLAYTIME—MESSING THINGS UP A LITTLE

Keep experimenting. Take time away from commissions, and use this time to really explore new ways of working. Bring new processes to your working pattern. If you normally draw from photographs, draw only from life; if you always create colors purely in Photoshop, scan lush colors, handpainted on watercolor paper.

TIP 39: WORKFLOW—KEEPING A ROUTINE IN YOUR LIFE

Structure your working day. It pays to recognize good working practice. Organize your time well, answer emails and open post at the start of every day, then get down to being creative. Anthony Burrill, illustrator/designer, explains why a structure helps his creative flow. "During the day I make and receive countless calls and emails. I am addicted to email, but sometimes have to turn it off to get rid of the distraction."

Part 05: Career Development

TIP 40: HOW TO BE AN ILLUSTRATOR WITHOUT LOSING YOUR SOUL

Enjoy what you do; it really is quite simple. Anthony Burrill, when asked about the lows of working in illustration, states, "I can't think of any." Others are more reflective. McFaul doesn't enjoy "the solitude," and Richard May warns, "cash flow can be a huge problem if you're not careful," but the illustrators at NCC say, "there are no lows."

TIP 41: JOB SATISFACTION— HOW TO SAY NO

Don't say yes to every job. Why would you say no? "Saying no and turning down work, and the money, can make you feel great, in charge," states Ian Wright. In the words of Michael Gillette, "I say no when I get a sinking feeling reading the brief and realize that doing the job will make me feel like a lesser artist," though he adds honestly, "This is sometimes negated by the need for cash."

TIP 42: SO YOU THINK YOU CAN TEACH? (1) GIVE SOMETHING BACK

Get involved with helping students. Away from the screen, the phone, and the solitude, many illustrators enjoy a regular teaching slot working with students. "Teaching reminds me why I wanted to be an illustrator

3

3.   Craig Ward, *Alphabet City*, personal project.

"I've been massively influenced by the 'symbolize and simplify' maxim of Fletcher and Bass, and I love to see a witty design that makes you smile when you get it."

Craig Ward

in the first place," admits Ian Wright. Austin at NEW states, "I think it's healthy. I like discussing ideas and meeting people who are excited at the prospect of doing new things, describing their world." Burgerman finds that giving lectures "makes me take stock of what I've actually done."

TIP 43: SO YOU THINK YOU CAN TEACH? (2) GETTING A JOB IN EDUCATION

Get a CV and samples of work together and send these to program leaders of foundation and undergraduate courses. Explain in a covering letter why you'd like to get involved, and offer to give a lecture about your own experiences to students. Perhaps start by contacting the very course you studied on.

TIP 44: YOUR PROFILE (1) BUILDING IT

Some illustrators crave peer recognition. For many, it isn't enough to have work regularly in print so they look to other methods and means of spreading their gospel. Speaking at conferences and live events, posting comments on discussion boards, and writing to magazines are all ways of getting your work in front of more people. But be careful not to overdo it—too much turns people off.

TIP 45: YOUR PROFILE (2) MAINTAINING IT

Keep clients aware of your latest work. This is a fundamental aspect of good marketing. A regular, email newsletter and press releases with information about recent projects will keep people informed. Again, too much and it'll have the opposite effect. "It kind of puts me off when I see people really hyping themselves," states JAKe. McFaul has his own advice. "If your website doesn't have a firm handshake, then the commissioner will be shaking the hands of others."

TIP 46: EXTRACURRICULAR ACTIVITIES

Exploit the overlap of illustration with other creative image-making skills. Careers in illustration are broader than ever before. McFaul believes the "boundaries between illustrators, designers, animators, artists, and photographers are long gone." The list of potential outputs continues to increase too. "I now like to do more of my own work and then find an outlet for it," explains Miles Donovan of Peepshow. "I just spent a month doing my own thing and then sold the lot to a T-shirt company in Japan."

TIP 47: EAT, DRINK, BREATHE ILLUSTRATION

Use your time wisely. If you're still at art school, use the facilities and expertise to their breaking point: you'll never get another chance. If you're out working in illustration ask yourself, "Am I giving it 100%? Do I want this more than anything?" Hard work and determination will pay off, but only if you have raw talent and a visual language that combines creativity, communication, and above all, originality.

TIP 48: ADVICE FROM THOSE IN THE KNOW

Illustration may be tough, but remember a few pearls of wisdom on dark days. "Try to keep a handle on what you enjoy about the process of image-making," offers Jody Barton. "Don't do anything half-heartedly," adds Austin at NEW. Patrick Thomas at laVista believes, "Your own projects and sketchbooks will feed your commercial work and help keep you sane." "Don't let the computer dictate what you do," warns Miles Donovan of Peepshow. Wise words indeed.

TIP 49: THE LAST WORD(S)

Illustration may be your entire world, but remember it isn't for everyone. "Keep things in perspective," Ian Wright advises. "Being paid to be creative isn't essential to the world's survival."

Case Study: The Promo Publication

1

2

"If you could do anything tomorrow, what would it be?" This simple question has elicited a huge response from an international audience of illustrators.

A beautifully simple idea, first mooted by a couple of design students in their penultimate year of study, *If you could do anything tomorrow – what would it be?* has elicited a tide of enthusiasm from illustrators keen to work to a brief that allows creative freedom, away from the restrictions of professional, paid projects.

Set up as an annual publication by Alex Bec and Will Hudson, *If you could …* aims to showcase the best in design and illustration, with contributions from both established and up-and-coming artists.

1. Alex Bec and Will Hudson, *If you could...* founders.
2. *If you could ...*, Ceri Amphlett illlustration for Issue One.
3. *If you could ...*, work from Issue One.
4. *If you could ...*, work from Issue One shown at the annual Village Fete, Victoria and Albert Museum, London

3

4

"The project was always about showcasing known and unknown artists," explains Bec, "as well as breaking boundaries and smashing the ego barrier, the idea being that anyone could submit."

The first publication, an A5 (148 × 210mm [c. $5^3/_4$ × $8^1/_4$in]) box set of 21 images, featured creations by many of the globe's leading illustrators—Michael Gillette, David Shrigley, Anthony Burrill, Ian Stevenson, Ian Wright, and Marion Deuchars—along with many new to the scene at the time, among them Will Ainley, Mr bingo, and Jim Stoten. Issue 1, launched in 2006 as a limited edition of 1,000, was featured in a number of design publications, and went on to become a very collectible item. It was sold online internationally as well as in art and design bookstores, galleries, and designer outlets across the UK and in the haven of all things designer, Colette, in Paris.

"The project was always about showcasing known and unknown artists," explains Bec, "as well as breaking boundaries and smashing the ego barrier, the idea being that anyone could submit." With a launch exhibition that featured the work of all contributors and a 2.5m (c. 8ft) wall space dedicated to encouraging the audience to respond in writing to the works, the show was designed to break the barrier between the artist and the audience.

Issue 2, published in the summer of 2007 and launched at exposure Gallery in London, was an even more adventurous affair—a 160-page, full-color, perfect-bound book, featuring over 110 images selected from a pool of around 400 submissions, again from around the globe. Hudson puts the project into perspective. "We've seen it as a good route into the industry," he admits. "We're always setting realistic, attainable goals, with determination, enthusiasm, and dependability."

Where Issue 3 goes is still very much up for discussion. "It might be a graduate only affair," says Bec. "We had some of the biggest names for Issue 2. It could be all unknowns next time." Watch their space.

5.   Victoria and Albert Museum, London, Village Fete.

6.   *If you could …*, Ian Stevenson illustration for Issue One.

7.   Publicity from the design industry for *If you could ….*

8.   *If you could …*, work from Issue One shown at the annual Village Fete, Victoria and Albert Museum, London.

7

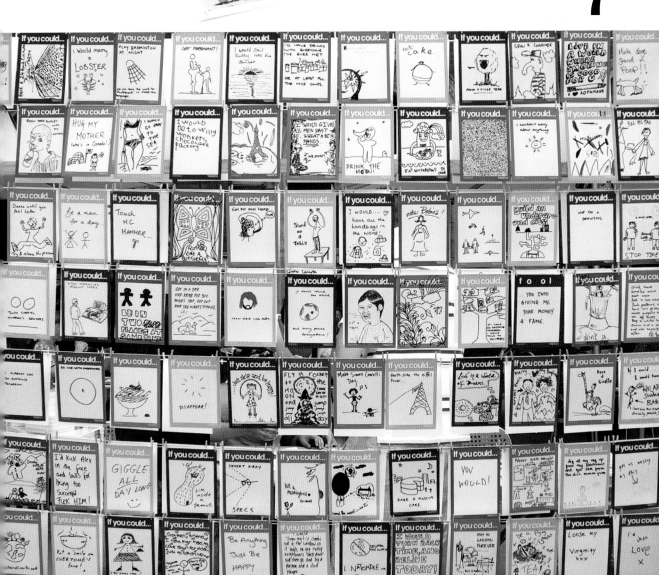

Tips for Generating Ideas

Creativity isn't a science, can't be relied upon to boot up at will, and will fail to ignite at the most crucial moments. Follow our advice to ensure that you remain the master of your own creativity.

If you have ever faced the blank sheet of paper or the blank screen with a blank brain—not a single creative idea forthcoming—you will know fear.

Perhaps the "fear" isn't quite what you would experience parachuting into enemy lines, or attempting to break the land speed record, and nobody ever lost an eye because they failed to find a creative solution in time to meet a deadline, but the sense of dread can be real enough.

While creative thinking isn't an exact science, there are, mercifully, a number of tips and tricks that can help kick-start a seized engine, extract some creative juices from a project, and lead you to your creative zenith. This is overstating it a touch perhaps, but when you hit the wall, these tips might just pull you through.

TIP 01: BLANK SCREEN/ BLANK CANVAS

Get yourself ready for action. Start a new project as you mean to go on; get rid of old papers, Post-it notes, and the remnants of previous projects before you embark on a new one. Clean your screen and keyboard, untangle cables, and place your thousands of hastily saved desktop files in their proper places. Create an uncluttered environment. Spending 30 minutes preparing your workspace will assist in preparing your "headspace" for creative thinking.

TIP 02: ENVIRONMENTAL ISSUES

Learn to recognize when and where you get your best ideas. Maximize your potential by tapping into your most creative environments. If you work well once you're deep in a project with music on max, but can't think clearly without silence, quit the music until you've got a "headfull" of thinking done. If your best work has come from ideas first conceived in a relaxed, carefree state of mind, create an oasis of calm away from work mode; shut out the landline, texts, and calls to your cell, and shut down email. It works.

TIP 03: BACK-OF-AN-ENVELOPE THINKING

However well planned your attempts at ensuring that a designated space—be that a prime location or a time slot—is perfectly set up, original ideas can hit at any time. Some of the greatest inventions are said to have begun life as sketches on the back of an envelope, pen and scrap paper being the first things that come to hand for the unprepared. Be ready for the onslaught of pure, unadulterated creative thinking by always having a notebook and pen, a digital camera, and even a Dictaphone to hand.

TIP 04: LAYOUTS OR SKETCHBOOKS

Choose whichever works best for you. There is an unwritten rule that at some point in the education of designers and artists there is a parting of the ways. Artists, and let's include illustrators in this description, tend to opt for the trusty sketchbook and pencil, while designers and art directors have always had a tendency to run for the layout pad and the felt-tipped pen. It doesn't matter one jot which tools you choose. Start thinking before you boot up and get some sense of your creative direction before Photoshop leads the way.

TIP 05: RESEARCH

Researching a new subject can offer new communication solutions, so go with the flow; chase new knowledge and use this to your advantage. Learning can provide the key to new thinking. One of the most influential aspects of a designer's or illustrator's working life is the truly inspirational subject matter that they are exposed to. A busy editorial illustrator, for instance, may have to tackle a commission about a hugely technical or scientific subject without any prior knowledge of it, and so get up-to-speed and become something of an expert about it in a hurry.

TIP 06: WORD ASSOCIATIONS

Don't always use images and visual solutions as a way of solving a communication problem. From time to time it pays dividends to start from a nonvisual perspective. Start by writing out words that spring to mind. Use a large sheet of white paper and a bold pen to make lists and connections. Alternatively, free your mind from any ideas and associations and just "dump" anything that comes into your head onto paper, however daft or unusable it may seem.

> "My life is spent obsessively searching for bits of paper and rubbish on the street; anything with a texture and a nice feel to it that I can collage into my work."

Tom Cornfoot

TIP 07: YOUR OWN PERSONAL REFERENCE LIBRARY

Don't rely on your local library for creative inspiration; create your very own reference library and never wait in line again. What the average citizen regards as trash is a potential creative gold mine for artists and designers. Collect used ticket stubs, old stamps, and manuals; buy secondhand and out-of-print books at garage sales; and begin to build your own unique reference archives. Find a format that works for you; scrapbooks and a glue stick, or box files with a carefully itemized index system—the choice is yours.

TIP 08: INSPIRATION VS. PERSPIRATION

Slaving away over a hot screen for hours/days/months isn't good for your creative output. Think of your creative mind as an engine; in order for it to run smoothly and efficiently, it requires oiling and topping up with fuel. So, step away from the computer and get out into the real world once in a while. Go get some inspiration. Check out events that you might normally ignore. See some modern dance, opera, sculpture, or take a short city break and visit flea markets and secondhand bookstores to add a new perspective to your life and work.

TIP 09: AGAINST THE CLOCK

If your ideas aren't always punctual and on track, plan your time carefully at the start of each new project—make space for research and ideas generation. For those occasions when this isn't feasible—commissions can arrive with little or no notice—develop a few surefire strategies. Use Google Image Search to start an inspirational journey. Key in words that spring to mind and combine this with a thesaurus to steer yourself to new places.

TIP 10: TESTING YOUR IDEAS

When the pressure is on, enlist the help of a colleague or friend to road test your ideas. If in doubt, test it out. We can all run into the problem of having a communication solution fall flat on its face. Why have a design solution rejected by a client because of a small detail you have overlooked, when it could so easily have been spotted by a fresh pair of eyes. Build this stage into a project timeline—finish the night before and look at it again in the morning with fresh eyes.

> "For illustration I always use my sketchbook and keep my drawings—they can be used for final artwork or as roughs to work up digitally." Mark Taplin

1. Tom Cornfoot, *Burlesque*, personal project.
2. Mark Taplin, *Erections like Steel*, poster.
3. *encore* magazine, Tez Humphreys, "Wake Up," editorial.

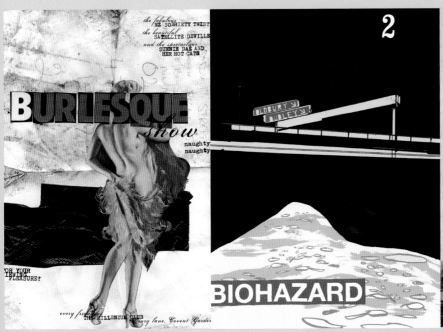

1

Tips for Surviving a Placement

Call it what you will, a placement, an internship, or work experience, it all boils down to one thing—a real chance to show what you are made of

1

It sounds like a win/win situation. Students wishing to enter the creative industries get real, firsthand experience of how it all works, while the design studio or advertising agency gets fresh-thinking, youthful enthusiasm, and can road test individuals for knock-down prices.

Whatever your views on the ethics of placements, there is no denying that they work. Getting your foot in the door can pay dividends. While a hot portfolio still counts, it's a cool-under-pressure personality that can make the difference in snaring that elusive first job offer. A placement can give you a platform on which to perform your magic.

"Clients are my most important thing, and it's always a frustration for them if I'm not precisely ready with my fees. So they come first." Karoly Kiralyfalvi

---

TIP 01: KNOW YOUR ONIONS
Before you even consider approaching a company, make it your business to find out as much about them as possible. Know their work, their clients, their standing in the industry, and know exactly why you would like to see yourself working for them. Read the design press, search websites; be prepared before you make any initial contact. Sarah Wall started a placement, leading to a real job after six months, at 3+Co in New York City, after graduating in the UK. Sarah advises, "Know your industry inside and out, be culturally aware, be a media junkie."

TIP 02: PREPARE YOUR ATTACK: PLAN WELL
It is vital that your first appearance make a distinct impression: you are up against many other people in a similar situation. Stand out from the crowd and make your offering count. Prepare a polished letter of introduction, CV, and work samples. These are your weapons. A poorly presented letter that falls down on standards of written English or has incorrect contact details will not impress. Sara Martin undertook a placement with Tony Chambers, Creative Director at *Wallpaper** magazine, which led to a real job. "Phone the company. Make sure you get the exact name and contact details," she advises.

TIP 03: INTERVIEWS— YOUR BIG CHANCE
Be sure to arrive in the locality of your interview early. Showing up even a few minutes late will look less than professional, and if you misjudge the time it takes on the subway or in traffic …. Arriving in good time will demonstrate keenness and professionalism before you've even opened your portfolio or your mouth. Suzy Wood, ex-Art Director at *Dazed & Confused* magazine and now at Studio Twenty, confesses to looking for "enthusiasm, an open mind, and a great attitude, and, oh yes, creativity," in placement students.

TIP 04: FIRST-DAY NERVES

Look sharp on your first day, as for your interview. It really pays to have put some thought into your appearance. Turn up looking like a student, and it's reasonable to assume that you'll be treated like a student rather than a hungry young professional. On arrival introduce yourself, and every time you're introduced to others at the company, memorize their names—know with whom you are working. "Lots of work opportunities come up through personal recommendation rather than job ads, so get yourself known quickly," advises Suzy Wood.

TIP 05: RULES OF THE GAME

A surefire way of waving a wand and turning a placement into a position is to become irreplaceable and indispensable. Take the initiative, offer to assist others, ask questions, make yourself beyond useful; don't be in the way or a burden. Riitta Ikonen, a graduate working at Syrup Helsinki in Finland, agrees. "Be active and involve yourself, ask anything and everything, be positive. If you don't feel interested or excited, you're in the wrong place." Sarah Wall in New York adds, "Be confident and be passionate about what you're doing."

TIP 06: 24/7

Demonstrate dedication and work hard, but remember, 24/7 is a state of mind and not a contractual requirement. The transition from breakfast in front of daytime TV to croissant and latte in front of the Creative Director can be an eye-opening experience. Dan Maughan undertook a three-month summer placement at Pentagram in Berlin while still a student, returning to the UK for his final year before starting a week-long placement at Pentagram in London. Offered a job at the end of that week, Dan believes, "I am where I am now largely because of working hard on that first placement."

TIP 07: INSPIRATION VS. PERSPIRATION

Make sure that you can contribute to the studio. It isn't a crime to make the coffee, but if that is the single most creative thing you've done all day, read the warning sign. According to Martin Andersen, Creative Director at Andersen M Studio, this is vital. "If the placement student is motivated, punctual, willing to experiment, they can be a real asset. They can really refresh the studio environment and introduce new ideas as well as making that really good cup of coffee on a stressful day," he states.

TIP 08: CLIENTS—MEETING AND GREETING

Designers can sometimes sound as though they're speaking a different language. Learn the lingo by attending client meetings, if you get the chance. Of course, you may not automatically be asked to attend, so just ask politely. Make sure that the creative team know you'll relish the experience, but will not speak out of turn. You'll get a better idea of deadlines, production details, and every aspect of a professional project, all of which is really useful. Dan Maughan, at Pentagram, hits home. "An insight into how the professional design world really works can't be gained in the classroom."

TIP 09: PAYMENT OR EXPENSES?

There is no general rule of thumb when it comes to how much or how little you'll be paid (or not) for a placement. Payment comes in spades—spades of experience that is. Expect to get enough cash for travel and lunch; that's a bus fare and a sandwich, not a cab and crab. Sarah Wall's pay for her first placement in New York tripled four weeks after she started, but as she says, "It's not unreasonable to work for nothing, so stop grumbling and extend that overdraft."

TIP 10: SIGNING OFF

Not all placements end with the holy grail of a job offer. In fact, most don't, but look at how you can increase your chances of being offered a job when one comes up in the future. Keep in contact with the company and start by writing to say just how much you enjoyed and learnt from the process. Not many interns bother to do this, so it might just make the difference. Send new samples of your work on a regular basis and invite key members of the company to your final-year exhibition. When it comes to placements remember, you have to be in it to win it.

1. Don't Panic Media, Karoly Kiralyfalvi, *Addiction Void*, poster.
2. *ROJO* magazine, Alex Robbins, "Otaku," editorial.

Riders

DATE

1   2 WEEKS

From
HOME
TO
PLACEMENT

RAIL FARE
$15.00

Case Study: The Collective

1

A collective with attitude, Black Convoy bends the rules of collaboration with projects that span publications, animations, and exhibitions in locations as far flung as London, New York, and Singapore.

2

Ask Black Convoy to give you the lowdown on how, when, and why it formed and you're likely to get as many answers as there are members—at last count around 12. The current lineup consists of Richard May, John McFaul, Adrian Johnson, Austin at NEW, Jon Burgerman, Lee Ford, Tim Marrs, Andy Potts, Steve at Neasden Control Centre, Mark Taplin, and recent recruit Holly Wales, the only female in this gang.

Creating an air of mystery and intrigue, more by accident than design, Black Convoy's beginnings have barely been documented. "Black Convoy rolled onto the scene in early 2004," begins Andy Potts, a paid-up, card-carrying member since Day One. "It was the brainchild, or love child, of Richard May and John McFaul. The idea

5

1. John McFaul and Tim Marrs at a Black Convoy collaboration show.
2. Wallpaper design.
3. Gorilla advertising in Singapore.
4. Flier for Black Convoy exhibition in Singapore.
5. Black Convoy exhibition in London.
6. Flier for Black Convoy exhibition.

was to bring together a ragtag team of like-minded illustrators and designers to work on the kind of projects we all wanted to go to town on—part inspiration and part self-indulgence," he recalls.

Pushed a little harder Potts admits, "It was just like one big mutual respect club, but we knew we were likely to generate some electricity." Electricity was certainly in the air. Following a few beer-fueled brainstorming sessions, a plan was hatched. With a launch exhibition at Seventeen in East London, closely followed by a trip to New York to work on a project with The Apartment (the creation of 15 large-format digital prints for a Swarovski-sponsored show), Black Convoy was on the move. A talk at an ICA (Institute of Contemporary Arts) event in London, put on by By Designers 4 Designers, was immediately followed with a trip to work on outdoor street art projects in Singapore for the Singapore Design Festival. Animation projects, further exhibitions, and work on a Black Convoy issue of *The Illustrated Ape* magazine, have ensured that the collective remains in demand.

Despite its interest in all things, Black Convoy likes to lay low and only appears on the scene when a specific project grabs its interest. "It's the need to join forces that brings us together," explains Austin at NEW. "To do something big, something good… Black Convoy is its own beast!" Richard May, cofounder, agrees. "You need a reason to exist. It's about power in numbers." Tim Marrs interjects, "I just love the projects that demand we all work directly onto walls. That's what it is all about—getting down and dirty and away from the everyday. It takes me out of my comfort zone."

Black Convoy projects are often hatched and schemed behind the screens of each collective member, deep within their own studios. Somehow ideas and themes start to take shape. An early press release cum mission statement for the group reads like the sleeve notes for a heavy metal album. "Emerging from the shadows of England's darkest cityscapes, crawling from the dry-ice fog of surburban wastelands, trailblazing outta Hellshire, come Black Convoy." It's a graphic image, but one that they all agree captures the essence of the team. In Tim Marrs' words, "It's all so sketchbook-like, raw, and fearless, with an emphasis on stripping images back. No bullshit, just in-your-face attitude."

It is left to Lee Ford to attempt an explanation of how projects see the light of day. "E-mails × 100. Panic! Another 100 e-mails or so. Draw, break, scan, saw, paint, draw, scan, print … Bingo!"

> "The idea was to bring together a ragtag team of like-minded illustrators and designers to work on the kind of projects that we all wanted to go to town on—part inspiration and part self-indulgence."

10

7. Hayward Gallery, London, still from an animation for Countervision exhibition.

8. Illustration by Andy Potts for Black Convoy.

9. Illustration by Mark Taplin and Andy Potts for Black Convoy.

10. *Black Convoy Machine.*

I STOPPED TO PULL A COUPLE OF PEOPLE OUT OF THE WATER BEFORE THEY WERE PLUNGED INTO THE RIVER, HEADED BACK THE WAY I'D COME, SOAKED TO THE SKIN, THEY STOPPED TO THANK ME BEFORE RUSHING AWAY, I GRABBED HOLD OF A THIRD BEFORE HE COULD ESCAPE. WHERE'S DR, JAIME GUZMAN? I YELLED, EYES WIDE WITH PANIC, THE SODDEN WHITE-COAT POINTED BACK TOWARDS THE BUILDING, BUT DON'T USE THE MAIN ENTRANCE, HE MUTTERED BEFORE HE TOO RAN OFF.

WELL, OBVIOUSLY.

I HEADED FOR THE SECOND CONCRETE BLOCK, WHICH APPEARED TO BE IN PRETTY GOOD SHAPE, THE DOOR WAS OPEN — THE SECURITY SYSTEM HAD EVIDENTLY FAILED, APART FROM A FOOT OF WATER EVERYWHERE, THE DRONE OF AN ALARM BELL AND THE OCCASIONAL SCREAM, IT WAS FINE, ALL THE SAME, I PULLED MY GUN FROM ITS HOLSTER AND FLIPPED THE SAFETY, IN SITUATIONS LIKE THIS, YOU NEVER CAN TELL.

THERE BEING NO SECURITY I HELPED MYSELF TO ANY DOOR I FANCIED, WANDERING DEEPER AND DEEPER INTO THE COMPLEX, CHOOSING ALWAYS THE DOORS MARKED 'RESTRICTED PERSONNEL ONLY'. I MANAGED TO FIND MYSELF IN SOME PART OF THE INSTALLATION WHICH WAS SEALED OFF FROM THE REST, EVEN THE ALARM SOUND FADED, INSTEAD, I HEARD THE FAINT STRAIN OF LATIN JAZZ, LISTENING CAREFULLY, I RECOGNISED IT AS CARLOS SANTANA'S RECORDING OF OYE COMO VA.

I CAME ACROSS MY SECRET INFORMANT JAIME GUZMAN, A MOMENT OR TWO LATER, HE DIDN'T SEEM A TINY BIT SURPRISED TO SEE ME, WE'D NEVER MET, BUT I'D TALKED TO HIM OVER A HIGHLY SECURED WEBCAM LINK, ASIDE FROM APPEARING A LITTLE FLUSTERED BY WHAT WAS CLEARLY A HEAVY DAY, JAIME LOOKED JUST THE SAME.

YOU'RE JUST IN TIME, HE SAID, GRABBING ME AT THE ELBOW AND DRAGGING ME INTO ANOTHER CHAMBER, HE SHOVED A DIVING MASK AND SNORKEL INTO MY HANDS, PULLED AN IDENTICAL PIECE OF KIT OVER HIS MOUTH AND NOSE AND SAID URGENTLY, 'COME ON' QUICKLY.

I REHOLSTERED MY GUN, DITCHED MY BACKPACK, JACKET AND SHOES AND FOLLOWED HIM TOWARDS THE SOUND OF SLOSHING WATER.

WE THOUGHT WE'D LOST IT. JAIME SAID BETWEEN GASPS AS

HE NODDED VIGOROUSLY, TEARS OF PRIDE SPRINGING TO HIS EYES.

I SWUM TO THE SURFACE, PULLED OFF MY MASK, SAID OKAY JAIME, WE'RE ALL DONE HERE.

JAIME'S FACE DROPPED, BUT WHY? DIDN'T YOU SEE? THAT CREATURE IS ABSOLUTELY, *TOTALLY UNPRECEDENTED IN THE WORLD OF OCEANOGRAPHY.

I SHOOK MY HEAD FIRMLY, I AND I WOULDN'T CARE, IT MAY BE SOME STRANGE FISH TO YOU, BUT TO ME IT'S JUST ANOTHER WHALE, LOOKS MOST LIKE ANY OTHER SEA CRITTER I'VE EVER SEEN, ALIEN BUDDY, SEEMS TO ME, YOU'VE BEEN HITTING THE SAUCE.

BUT THE VOICE LISTEN CAN'T YOU HEAR?

I PUT MY HEAD INTO THE WATER AND LISTENED, SURE ENOUGH, THERE IT WAS, THE LOW, BARELY TUNEFUL AND DEEP, LOWING TONES OF THE WHALE.

OOOOOYYEE OOOOMOOO YAAAAAA..

A SINGING WHALE? PLEASE, ANY HUMPBACK CAN DO BETTER, IT DIDN'T EVEN ENUNCIATE THE C

LIKE EVERY LAST CASE I EVER INVESTIGATED, FOR ALL THE INITIAL EXCITEMENT, IT ENDED WITH DISAPPOINTMENT, BUT I TELL YOU THIS: BY SOME CRAZY TRICK OF MEMORY, THE SOUND OF THAT WHALESONG HAS GOTTEN ITSELF STUCK IN MY HEAD, EVEN TO THIS DAY, I CAN'T SHAKE IT.

8

9

Tips for Keeping Clients Happy

No more "Don't get mad, get even." Keep your clients smiling with a bright and cheerful new you. "Don't worry; be happy."

Keeping clients happy is a job in itself. You can be the hottest designer in town, creating the coolest work this side of SoHo or Soho, but without a little insider knowledge on keeping your clients smiling, it can all go pear-shaped.

Whether you describe what you do as graphic design, photography, illustration, animation, or commercial art, it is based upon communication. You are a visual communicator, but in order to succeed in creating a warm glow within your client each time your name is mentioned, you'll need all-round communication skills.

You'll need to have the know-how to juggle impossible impending deadlines, hardware failures, software crashes, and creative brick walls, on top of the often highly pressurized task of creating stunning work (remind me why we are in this line of work), and all while maintaining a friendly oasis of inner calm and outward positivity.

1. Si Scott, *Butterfly*, personal project.
2. Alice Stevenson, *Ark*, personal project.
3. Maxwell Paternoster, *Defish Lung*, personal project.

1

TIP 01: DELIVER ON TIME
Delivering on time is the most important requirement in keeping a client happy. You can charge great fees, always be polite, invite clients around for coffee and bagels, but all of that will count for nothing if you fail to deliver projects to your clients on schedule. This is no time for lame "but the dog ate my homework" tales. This is real life, with real deadlines, and no excuse will cut the mustard. Deliver on your delivery agreements and you'll have a happy client, or at the very least you'll have one that isn't angry.

TIP 02: BE REASONABLE
So you can deliver your projects to clients within the specified deadline. Now you're really up and running. But don't take anything for granted; getting the work done on time is a given, not a luxury for most clients. You need to crank up a gear if you want to establish a great and continuing working relationship. The answer is, be reasonable, be gracious, and above all else be a warm and wonderful human being. Being polite in person and on the phone can really pay dividends. Who wants to work with a grouch?

TIP 03: BE PROFESSIONAL
There is never an excuse for being less than professional if you want to stay the right side of your client. Being professional should be part and parcel of the service you offer. Think about it. You're less than pleased if given service that doesn't reach your expectations, and even if they don't complain directly to you, your clients can and will quietly leave if your levels of professionalism fall below par.

TIP 04: ASK QUESTIONS
A client likes a designer who is informed about and interested in a project. When you attend a briefing session with a client, be interested, be motivated, and be sure to equip yourself with the information and knowledge you'll need to get the project underway. Your client has a visual communication issue to solve, and you're the person to solve it, but only if you really understand the issues. Get behind the scenes, really get to grips with the problems that the client is facing—only then can you actually start designing.

TIP 05: DON'T DEMAND THE IMPOSSIBLE

The punk/Situationist saying, "Be reasonable. Demand the Impossible," might be a great mantra to follow when working for yourself, but it won't help you win clients. Your client has a life too and they, at least nine times out of ten, prefer an easygoing one to a stressed-out one. Try to make life easy for them. Don't call with a thousand questions at 5.25pm on a hot Friday evening: they want out of the office and into the pub. Don't scream at them down the phone line or send expletives via email because they've forgotten to call. Chill out.

TIP 06: DON'T OVERCHARGE

Do you know anyone who likes to be ripped off, or pay over the odds for something that they know they could have got cheaper elsewhere? Don't undersell yourself—keep your fees level with your experience and track record—but at the same time don't raise them just because you think a client might pay. A client might agree to a higher fee than usual if they have a deadline to meet and finding another designer is tricky in the time frame. But guess what? They'll have found another designer before the next job is ready to commission.

TIP 07: KEEP IN TOUCH

Keeping in touch costs nothing. Well, not exactly nothing, but not a lot more. A card at Christmas, a change-of-address card at the right time … That kind of thing costs only the price of a stamp, and the card of course. Whatever the financial outlay, sending a card sends the message that you care about your client. A huge and tacky calendar may seem like a cheap marketing ploy, keeping your name on the wall of your client throughout the year is generally seen as a gimmick, but a business card handed over at the right time can work wonders.

TIP 08: THAT PERSONAL TOUCH

How frustrating is it to get a series of recorded options when you need to speak to a real person about a real problem? Your client will need to speak with you on a regular basis. They'll assume that their project is the only one on your screen constantly, so keeping lines of communication open is a necessity, not a luxury. Use an answer-phone service, record a friendly message yourself, return calls and emails promptly and courteously, and clients will grin rather than frown. Communication is your business after all.

TIP 09: LOOK SMART, THINK SMART

Dressing the part is important. How you turn up to client meetings is crucial. If you can't present yourself well, how can your client trust that you'll present their project well? So your style may be more jeans and T-shirt than cravat and spats, but however you dress, make sure you're clean and tidy. Don't arrive looking like you've been up all night, either at a club or working on their project. Brush your hair, brush your teeth, and brush up your act.

TIP 10: GIVE IT SOME ATTITUDE

How clients perceive you and your working methods is down to your overall attitude. A bad attitude gives a bad impression and is completely unnecessary. You can and should maintain a cheerful, professional approach at all times. You are stressed, overworked, and underpaid, and the clients-from-hell are changing their minds every three minutes; smile, be positive, and feel at one with the world, or at least try.

Tips for Negotiating Fees

One of the toughest aspects of working solo or as part of a start-up within the creative industry is understanding fee structures and negotiating the best deal.

There are no magic wands, no secret formulae to apply, no published facts on the subject of fee negotiation for humble designers and illustrators to follow—until now, that is.

"What is your fee?" is the question many creatives fear. There seems to be an unfathomable chasm between the artistic and creative mind-set and the astute mind of those with a real grip on their financial worth. How can it be so tricky to fully comprehend what a design project is worth?

A simple mistake in quoting for a project can break you. A design commission can move rapidly from a healthy and relatively stress-free project to one that drags you down like a lead weight. Make no bones, it may not be the easiest aspect of the job, but getting it right is crucial to the success of a business.

TIP 01: QUOTING (1) SETTING FEES
Sometimes a client knows exactly how much cash they have to spend and they cut, or ask you to cut their cloth accordingly. This no-holds-barred, honest, straightforward approach is about as rare as four-leaf clovers. For all other situations, rely on a good dose of common sense and/or previous experience to inform you of the financial worth of different projects. And if these fail, request some time to consider your fee, then get on the phone and ask around for advice.

TIP 02: QUOTING (2) WHEN TO QUOTE
Knowing when to quote and when to just ask what the budget is is never easy. Some clients play their hand close to their chests and won't divulge their budget. Jasper Goodall, an illustrator represented by Big Active, recommends the following technique when going for the kill. "Go in high and when the client freaks out at the price, ask what the budget for the job really is." It might be a risky route to take though, and Goodall agrees. "Of course, if they just agree to your fee without question, that's when you really want to kick yourself."

TIP 03: QUOTING (3) HOW TO QUOTE
It is always much easier to offer a fee through a written quotation than it is to do it face-to-face. You don't have to stare into the whites of the client's eyes, and you have the opportunity to explain clearly what the costs are and how they relate to the project. Martin Andersen of Andersen M Studio explains. "Itemize everything you design so there are no gray areas. The number of times I've created work for a record company only to see them reuse it without permission or payment is frightening."

TIP 04: QUOTING (4) A SLIDING SCALE
Bob Gordon, author of *The Complete Guide to Digital Graphic Design*, has a simple piece of advice. "Find out what kind of car your client drives when evaluating just how much to charge." Siobhan Keaney, D&AD award-winning designer, advises to "simply think of a number and then double it" when trying to calculate a fee. Jokes apart, be flexible, be prepared to adjust your fee to suit the size of the client, and you'll not go far wrong. Remember, a charity will always have less to spend than a multinational.

TIP 05: AGENTS—WHY THEY CAN PAY DIVIDENDS
Most people have some gripe against agents. While some may appear less than scrupulous in their dealings, they can have their uses. Agents can command higher fees for a job. Clients generally understand that working through an agency, when commissioning an illustrator or a photographer, will cost a little more. Agents also have a wealth of experience gained through quoting on a daily basis, and they don't get emotionally tied up in a project. In essence, the more they get for you, the more they get for themselves.

TIP 06: PITCH FEES—HOW AND WHEN TO COMMAND ONE
Pitches are an everyday fact for many designers. They provide an opportunity to present ideas and design approaches to a client, and allow the client to make an informed decision about who they work with. They also mean you get a taste of a project before getting in too deep. However, they are work, so make sure you receive a fee. Be firm, quote a daily rate, and make it clear that this fee does not give them the rights to reproduce or use the work in any commercial way.

TIP 07: FREEBIES—SHOULD YOU/SHOULDN'T YOU?
Illustrator Michael Gillette states up front, "Never work for no fee. The client must pay." Ian Wright, illustrator with ZeegenRush, is equally adamant. "Make it your company policy to never work for nothing." But he admits that when starting out this can be an issue that is put to the test. Make sure that you are happy with the

arrangement and put an agreement in place even if no money is changing hands. Perhaps they can pay in other ways: free books, records, publicity, etc.

TIP 08: WHEN BUDGETS COLLIDE—CAUSE AND EFFECT

Be careful. There is a very fine line between a budget and a fee, and you must work to ensure that the two sides exist in harmony. If you're given a budget for a project, it may include financial provision for a number of aspects of production as well as including your fee. Handle this wisely. Ensure that you get the best from your budget and don't overspend: this may well have to be paid from the proportion that is your fee. Check prices, extras, and delivery costs, and maintain a spreadsheet: costs do add up.

TIP 09: USAGE—HOW THIS AFFECTS FEES

Where, and for how long your work is used can dictate the fee. Illustrator Jasper Goodall has a simple formula. "Duration + media = fee." Fellow illustrator Gary Powell agrees. "Make sure you clarify the usage or you'll be the one being used." A rule of thumb worth remembering is: the wider the usage and the longer the campaign, the higher the fee. While you may take as long to create an illustration for a small publisher as you do to design a billboard poster, you'll earn more for the ad job.

TIP 10: WHEN TO RAISE FEES

There comes a point in everyone's career when they feel the time is right to ask for a pay rise. Working for yourself is no different, and after you've proven your worth to one or two clients, you can propose an increase in your fees. Do this professionally. Don't just whack your next invoice up by 20%—explain verbally or in writing why you're charging more. Perhaps you're offering a wider service, you've had to expand, or you started at a lower rate with an understanding that fees would increase over time. It is worth recognizing that a fee increase for some clients will be out of the question—they'll always look for something cheaper!

"I try to keep self-authored projects running alongside commercial projects."

Andy Smith

1

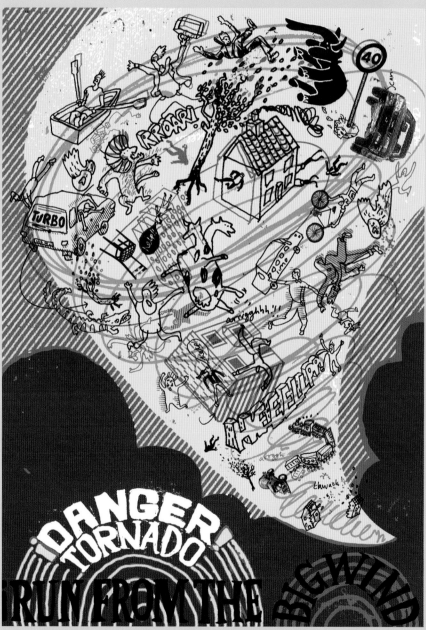

1.   Andy Smith, *Big Wind*, personal project.

Tips for Winning Awards

Want to win an award? Keen to experience the thrill of the podium, champagne corks popping, and the sound of the flashbulb going off?

Doesn't everyone secretly dream of stepping out of a limo, sweeping up the red carpet, making a grand entrance, then delivering a gushing acceptance speech before punching the air with a glittering award in one hand and a giant check in the other? Don't they?

While awards ceremonies in Hollywood have a certain something that is generally missing from the kind of prize-giving events that graphic designers, illustrators, animators, and other members of the mere-mortal design community have, the opportunity to attend, and recognition for being at the top of your game, does give you a certain buzz.

If you want recognition for your achievements, if you fancy being the one who fellow designers aspire to be, picking up awards won't do your quest any harm. Here we cover the tips for how to get your name in the annuals.

TIP 01: BE IN IT TO WIN IT

The first and most important piece of advice about winning awards is that you have to be in it to win it. It really is as simple as that. In order to have your work judged best in show, you'll need to enter it into awards and competitions. It is a fact that the designers who bitch and complain about who won what and who should have won what and how their own work would easily have won are the designers who never get their act together to actually enter.

TIP 02: CHOOSING THE RIGHT AWARDS TO ENTER

D&AD, RSA, AOI … the list goes on. All design organizations have competitions, some just for students, some for recent graduates, some for industry hot shots. Once you start looking, you'll see there are numerous awards just waiting for your entry. Get in touch with organizations. Check their websites to get up-to-the-minute details on competitions and awards. If you're a student, keeping a keen eye on bulletin boards around the campus will elicit more information. Of course, keep your eyes peeled on publications covering digital art and illustrations, such as *Computer Arts*, published worldwide every month: many awards are listed within their pages.

TIP 03: WHEN NOT TO BEND THE RULES

You'd be surprised how many people enter competitions only to find their entries null and void because they haven't followed the requirements to the letter. Take the time to read these carefully, and follow them. Some applications require a fee just to enter the competition; others require a hanging fee, payable if your work is selected as part of the competition exhibition; yet others require a publication fee, payable if your work is selected to be published in an annual. Negotiating these fees can be a minefield.

1

"The last job I had was so awful, it made me absolutely determined to succeed on my own, so that really spurred me on to find success as an illustrator and animator."

Mr bingo

2

1. Colette, Jeremyville, *Just Keep Movin'*, exhibition poster.
2. Dorling Kindersley, Mr bingo, *One Dollar*, book illustration.

TIP 04: PRESENTATION, PRESENTATION, PRESENTATION

"Good presentation is never recognized, but bad presentation can let down the whole deal." This is so true. Join a judging panel to see the reaction to poorly presented work. It's not pretty. Don't send in second-rate printouts, don't scribble out handwritten entry labels or mount work on chocolate-colored board more suited to a display at the local town fair. Do the right thing and up the stakes by ensuring that your work looks the very best that it can. Invest time, energy, and some cash to make sure your application receives the attention it deserves.

TIP 05: CONCEPT OVER CONTENT/STYLE OVER SUBSTANCE

If you know that D&AD is searching for genius creative talent, a project packed full of great ideas and great craftsmanship, make sure you submit work that fulfills this brief and is not just eye candy. If Adobe is looking for a fantastically creative use of its software applications, there is little point in submitting work created using letterpress. It really pays to understand the competition you are entering and what its requirements are. Don't waste your entry fees by being uninformed. A little knowledge can go a long way.

TIP 06: STAYING IN THE PUBLIC EYE

Winning competitions gets your work in view of the right people. This can be crucial in garnering new commissions for exciting projects, an offer of a new job, or a step up the career ladder. While it is fun being part of the "in crowd" when you take your place on the winner's podium, you need to take stock of your newfound position in the cold light of day. Having your work recognized and receiving accolades are cool, but ensure that they really mean something; capitalize on your success.

TIP 07: THEY'LL BE THE JUDGE

Judges are only looking for one thing—the very best! How they get to their final decision can be an arduous and long-winded process. Getting a D&AD jury to agree on an award-winning ad campaign is a tough job, and selecting a great illustration from hundreds of AOI (Association of Illustrators) entries can be painful, but there's no secret to getting it right as an entrant. All you can do is submit your best work and leave it to the judges to select what they will. It's in the lap of the gods.

TIP 08: THAT WINNING FEELING

As Norman Cook, aka Fat Boy Slim (or at least Red Design's award-winning sleeve for his album) states, "I'm No. 1 so why try harder?" Picking up awards can feel just great. Like collecting a gold star from your teacher at the age of five, heading up to the stage and collecting a well-deserved award is a wonderful experience, but don't let the success go to your head. Too many winners become a touch too cocky and feel that the world owes them a living. It doesn't.

TIP 09: GO GLOBAL

Awards and competitions are a global issue, and they will not just arrive on your doorstep. If you are hungry to win and are happy to go to greater geographical lengths to satisfy your cravings, then you might like to look a little further. Check out the major design centers around the world. Use the web to find out what's happening in New York, Tokyo, Berlin, Hong Kong, Melbourne; the likelihood is that you'll find numerous competitions and awards schemes looking for international entries.

TIP 10: JUST DO IT

Awards and accolades may be the icing on the cake of a perfect career, but the everyday reality for the jobbing designer or illustrator is a somewhat different tale. For every award-winning piece of design, there are hundreds of equally strong projects. For many designers, creating great work that communicates and fulfills the brief, and working for appreciative clients, can be the best prize there is. Do the best work you can, and only when you've done that, submit the work for awards.

Will Ainley
www.willainley.co.uk

Emily Alston
www.emilyforgot.co.uk

Ceri Amphlett
www.ceriamphlett.co.uk

Sanna Annukka
www.sanna-annukka.com

Richard Ardagh
www.elephantsgraveyard.co.uk

Craig Atkinson
www.craigatkinson.co.uk

Sasha Barr
www.thisisthenewyear.com

Jody Barton
www.jodybarton.co.uk

Thomas Barwick
www.thomasbarwick.com

Luke Best
www.lukebest.com

Mr bingo
www.mr-bingo.co.uk

Paul Blow
www.paulblow.com

Christian Borau
www.caoscc.com

Jenny Bowers
www.jennybowers.co.uk

Todd Breland
www.toddalanbreland.com

Jon Burgerman
www.jonburgerman.com

Paul Burgess
www.mrpaulburgess.com

Anthony Burrill
www.anthonyburrill.com

C'est Moi Ce Soir
www.cestmoicesoir.com

Brian Cairns
www.briancairns.com

Graham Carter
www.graham-carter.co.uk

Naja Conrad-Hansen
www.meannorth.com

Tom Cornfoot
www.tomcornfoot.co.uk

Gemma Correll
www.gemmacorrell.com

Nathan Daniels
www.nathandaniels.com

Paul Davis
www.copyrightdavis.com

Chris Dent
www.chrisdent.co.uk

Marion Deuchars
www.mariondeuchars.com

Miles Donovan
www.milesdonovan.co.uk

Faile
www.faile.net

Barry Falls
www.barryfalls.com

Peter Field
www.peterjamesfield.co.uk

David Foldvari
www.davidfoldvari.co.uk

Jason Ford
www.heartagency.com

Lee Ford
www.leeford.org

Pete Fowler
www.monsterism.net

Melvin Galapon
www.mynameismelvin.co.uk

Tom Gauld
www.cabanonpress.com

Michael Gillette
www.michaelgillette.com

Jasper Goodall
www.jaspergoodall.com

Josh Gosfield
www.joshgosfield.com

Matthew Green
www.icantbelieveitsnotbetter.com

Eleanor Grosch
www.pushmepullyoudesign.com

Karin Hagen
www.karinhagen.com

Phil Hankinson
www.heartagency.com

Hennie Haworth
www.henniehaworth.co.uk

Adam Hayes
www.mrahayes.co.uk

Nick Higgins
www.nickhiggins.co.uk

Tim Hill
www.bivouac1927.blogspot.com

Tez Humphreys
www.glufolio.co.uk

Oliver Hydes
www.oliverhydes.com

ilovedust
www.ilovedust.com

Insect
www.insect.co.uk

Rosie Irvine
www.rosieirvine.com

Ryu Itadani
www.ryuitadani.com

Keiji Ito
www.site-ufg.com

JAKe
www.jake-art.com

Billie Jean
www.billiejean.co.uk

Jeremyville
www.jeremyville.com

Adrian Johnson
www.adrianjohnson.org.uk

Karoly Kiralyfalvi
www.extraverage.net

Tatsuro Kiuchi
www.tatsurokiuchi.com

Yuko Kondo
www.yukokondo.com

Seijiro Kubo
www.butterfly-stroke.com

Joel Lardner
www.joellardner.com

Joe Magee
www.periphery.co.uk

Marine
www.hellomarine.com

Tim Marrs
www.timmarrs.co.uk

Mick Marston
www.thefutilevignette.com

Andy Martin
www.andy-martin.com

Asako Masunouchi
www.asako-masunouchi.com

Richard May
www.art-dept.com/illustration/may/index.
html

Neil McFarland
www.parishair.com

McFaul
www.mcfaul.net

Joe McLaren
www.joemclaren.com

Daniel Mitchell
www.daniel-mitchell.co.uk

Kate Mockford
www.katemockford.com

Christian Montenegro
www.christianmontenegro.com.ar

Patrick Morgan
www.patrickmorgan.co.uk

Mutador
www.mutador.com

MWM Graphics
www.mwmgraphics.com

George Myers
www.georgemyers.co.uk

Neasden Control Centre
www.neasdencontrolcentre.com

Peter Nencini
www.peternencini.co.uk

NEW
www.new-online.co.uk

Martin O'Neil
www.cutitout.co.uk

Simon Oxley
www.idokungfoo.com

Ayşegül Özmen
www.bepositivedesign.net

Maxwell Paternoster
www.maxwellp.co.uk

Simon Pemberton
www.simonpemberton.com

Pietari Posti
www.pposti.com

Andy Potts
www.andy-potts.com

Corinna Radcliffe
www.corinnaradcliffe.com

Andrew Rae
www.andrewrae.org.uk

Shonagh Rae
www.heartagency.com

Paul Reilly
www.art-dept.com/illustration/reilly/index.
html

Andy Rementer
www.andyrementer.com

Alex Robbins
www.alexrobbins.co.uk

Kerry Roper
www.youarebeautiful.co.uk

Laurie Rosenwald
www.rosenworld.com

Brett Ryder
www.brettryder.co.uk

Edvard Scott
www.edvardscott.com

Si Scott
www.siscottdesign.com

Serge Seidlitz
www.sergeseidlitz.com

Natsko Seki
www.natsko.com

Nicholas Sheehy
www.showchicken.com

Andy Smith
www.asmithillustration.com

David Sparshott
www.davidsparshott.com

Alice Stevenson
www.alicestevenson.com

Ian Stevenson
www.ilikedrawing.co.uk

Jim Stoten
www.jimtheillustrator.co.uk

Richard Stow
www.gingerbeards.com

Fiodor Sumkin
www.sumkin.opera78.com

TADO
www.tado.co.uk

Kam Tang
www.kamtang.co.uk

Mark Taplin
www.taplabs.com

Elliott Thoburn
www.elliotthoburn.co.uk

Studio Tonne
www.studiotonne.com

Junichi Tsuneoka
www.stubbornsideburn.com

Uncompressed
www.uncompressed.be

Aude Van Ryn
www.heartagency.com

Vault49
www.vault49.com

Lucy Vigrass
www.lucyvigrass.co.uk

Holly Wales
www.eatjapanesefood.co.uk

Craig Ward
www.wordsarepictures.co.uk

Paul Wearing
www.paulwearing.co.uk

Alex Williamson
www.alexwilliamson.co.uk

Spencer Wilson
www.spencerwilson.co.uk

Steve Wilson
www.wilson2000.com

Matt Wingfield
www.mattwingfieldstudio.com

Ian Wright
www.mrianwright.co.uk

Index

Acknowledgments

Dedication
This book is dedicated to Lesley Zeegen

Special Thanks
I would like to thank the following people for their support, patience, and understanding:

Lesley, Louie, Jake, and Felix Zeegen
Russell Hrachovec at compoundEye
Ben Schmit at compoundEye
Karen Norquay, Sarah Elliott, Margaret Huber, and all the staff in the Graphic Design and Illustration Department and the Research Department at the University of Brighton
Ondrej Slezek
Oliver Hydes at Square Enough
Helen Rush and Nicki Field at ZeegenRush
Dorothée Fritze
Lindy Dunlop, Luke Herriott, Tony Seddon, and April Sankey at RotoVision

Contributors
Many thanks to all the talented people who kindly contributed their work and time:

Will Ainley, Emily Alston, Ceri Amplett, Sanna Annukka, Richard Ardagh, Craig Atkinson, Sasha Barr, Jody Barton, Thomas Barwick, Luke Best, Mr bingo, Paul Blow, Christian Borau, Jenny Bowers, Todd Breland, Jon Burgerman, Paul Burgess, Anthony Burrill, C'est Moi Ce Soir, Brian Cairns, Graham Carter, Naja Conrad-Hansen, Tom Cornfoot, Gemma Correll, Nathan Daniels, Paul Davis, Chris Dent, Marion Deuchars, Miles Donovan, Faile, Barry Falls, Peter Field, David Foldvari, Jason Ford, Lee Ford, Pete Fowler, Melvin Galapon, Tom Gauld, Michael Gillette, Jasper Goodall, Josh Gosfield, Matthew Green, Eleanor Grosch, Karin Hagen, Phil Hankinson, Hennie Haworth, Adam Hayes, Nick Higgins, Tim Hill, Tez Humphreys, Oliver Hydes, ilovedust, Insect, Rosie Irvine, Ryu Itadani, Keiji Ito, JAKe, Billie Jean, Jeremyville, Adrian Johnson, Karoly Kiralyfalvi, Tatsuro Kiuchi, Yuko Kondo, Seijiro Kubo, Joel Lardner, Joe Magee, Marine, Tim Marrs, Mick Marston, Andy Martin, Asako Masunouchi, Richard May, Neil McFarland, McFaul, Joe McLaren, Daniel Mitchell, Kate Mockford, Christian Montenegro, Patrick Morgan, Mutador, MWM Graphics, George Myers, Neasden Control Centre, Peter Nencini, NEW, Martin O'Neil, Simon Oxley, Aysegül Özmen, Maxwell Paternoster, Simon Pemberton, Pietari Posti, Andy Potts, Corinna Radcliffe, Andrew Rae, Shonagh Rae, Paul Reilly, Andy Rementer, Alex Robbins, Kerry Roper, Laurie Rosenwald, Brett Ryder, Edvard Scott, Si Scott, Serge Seidlitz, Natsko Seki, Nicholas Sheehy, Andy Smith, David Sparshott, Alice Stevenson, Ian Stevenson, Jim Stoten, Richard Stow, Fiodor Sumkin, TADO, Kam Tang, Mark Taplin, Elliott Thoburn, Studio Tonne, Junichi Tsuneoka, Uncompressed, Aude Van Ryn, Vault49, Lucy Vigrass, Holly Wales, Craig Ward, Paul Wearing, Alex Williamson, Spencer Wilson, Steve Wilson, Matt Wingfield, Ian Wright